Say This,
Not That

JEREMY P. TARCHER/PENGUIN

a member of Penguin Group (USA)

New York

Say This, Not That

A FOOLPROOF GUIDE TO

EFFECTIVE INTERPERSONAL

COMMUNICATION

Carl Alasko, Ph.D.

JEREMY P. TARCHER/PENGUIN
Published by the Penguin Group
Penguin Group (USA) LLC
375 Hudson Street
New York, New York 10014

USA · Canada · UK · Ireland · Australia
New Zealand · India · South Africa · China

penguin.com
A Penguin Random House Company

Most Tarcher/Penguin books are available at special-quantity discounts for bulk purchase for sales
promotions, premiums, fund-raising, and educational needs. Special books or book excerpts also
can be created to fit specific needs. For details, write: Special.Markets@us.penguingroup.com.

Library of Congress Cataloging-in-Publication Data

Alasko, Carl.
Say this, not that: a foolproof guide to effective interpersonal communication / Carl Alasko.
p.   cm.
ISBN 978-1-58542-932-5
1. Interpersonal communication.   2. Interpersonal relations.   3. Conflict management.   I. Title.
BF637.C45A42   2014   2013037081
153.6—dc23

Printed in the United States of America
1   3   5   7   9   10   8   6   4   2

Book design by Gretchen Achilles

Contents

PART THREE
Parenting: Don't Say That to Your Kid ... Instead Say This

PART FOUR
Friendships: Voluntary Relationships That Make Life Better

PART FIVE
Say This ... in the Workplace

PART SIX
Everyday Situations

Say This,
Not That

How to Use This Book

Well, what *should* I say?" he asks.

"It's useless trying to talk to him," she complains.

"If I try to say anything, we end up in a fight!" he grumbles.

Saying the right words is not easy. Sometimes it seems impossible. That's why I wrote this guide to straight talk—to help you say the right words in the right way at the right time.

Just as important, this guide can help you stop saying the *wrong* words—ones that make things worse.

•——•

Twenty-five years of working as a psychotherapist with individuals and couples who struggle to communicate their feelings and ideas have taught me that people need direct guidance about how to choose the right words.

During my earlier years as a therapist, I had been taught to practice "clinical objectivity." My task was to remain neutral as patients sought to gain insights into their motives.

Some twenty years ago, for instance, when a couple like Kathy and Robb would arrive for their therapy session in a visibly agitated state and Kathy's first words would be an angry, "Robb, why did you forget to call me? Can't you remember anything?" I would have asked her a *clinically neutral* question such as, "Kathy, how do you imagine Robb feels when you say that?"

Since then, I've learned that actually, in that moment, Kathy doesn't give a hoot about how Robb feels. She's frustrated and angry, her pulse rate is elevated, her blood vessels have constricted, she's ready for a fight and has no desire for resolution.

She's after emotional blood.

So these days, in similar situations, I jump right into the middle and say firmly: *"Kathy, don't say that to Robb.* All you'll do is get him angry, and then he'll just want to get even."

Confronted with this directly, Kathy will usually ask, "Well, what *should* I say when he . . . ?"

I tell her to say this: " *'I'm upset that you didn't call me.'* Nothing more. Just that."

Then I'll discuss with both of them why those few simple words—nothing more—make a whole lot of sense.

Why do they make sense? Because when someone is already agitated, further confrontation only pumps up the tension and primes everyone for battle.

That's the core question this book addresses: *What to say in stressful moments.*

In the following pages, I'll explain how to carefully choose words and—equally important—adopt nonthreatening gestures. Each two-page scene will demonstrate the difference between words that will start another conflict that pushes you further away from happiness, or help create a successful interaction that leads to more intimacy. Or at least to better results.

———•———

Let's look deeper into the biology behind communication success or failure.

All of the scenes in this book are based on the following biological fact:

We are all hardwired to react instantly to a physical or verbal attack.

Everyone is programmed with the fight/flight syndrome that instantly floods the bloodstream with adrenaline. This hardwiring is not a choice. Within seconds we're primed to either fight like mad or run like hell. Our heart and muscles are ready for action—**not** for thinking.

No one escapes this basic human program.

So while we have learned over the millennia to control our physical reactions (our tendency toward violence), we have a much harder time controlling our words.

In fact, when you're sufficiently excited, provoked, confused, fearful or embarrassed, you often can't think at all because *the thought process itself* often fails.

Anger and fear quickly take over. Your impulse is to get even by inflicting immediate pain on whoever is causing *you* pain. Pressured by your frustrations, anxieties, irritations and resentments, you say something sarcastic, critical or accusatory that only makes things worse by creating yet more conflict.

Conflict erodes emotional trust—the lifeblood of every successful relationship.

———•———

So how *do* you control what you say in such situations? How *can* you avoid spilling emotional blood?

You avoid it by having sensible responses *already prepared* for use in potentially out-of-control situations. By rehearsing in advance. And by memorizing specific guidelines of what to say when you're feeling pressure or you're upset. Rehearsing a response can make all the difference in everyday interactions such as:

- Your boyfriend has left a mess in the kitchen . . . again!
- You order a special gift for your sister and she barely notices your effort.
- Your wife wonders why you're too "dense" to remember something she's told you.
- You try your best to be helpful to a friend but she ignores you.
- A coworker says something demeaning that implies you're incompetent.
- A relative criticizes an ambitious holiday meal you've just prepared.

Knowing how to respond in the best possible way in any of these situations can make the difference between ending up feeling stronger, more self-assured, more connected and more competent—as opposed to feeling disconnected, criticized and incapable.

There's another vitally important factor in successful communication: *how* you express your words. When speaking face-to-face, you engage your entire body. Posture, gestures, facial expressions, tone of voice, and inflection—these all support or distort your words' impact.

For that reason, many scenes in the book also contain tips on making sure that your nonverbal communication will make your words as effective as possible. You'll find those woven into the suggested answers.

Each scene poses a scenario and possible responses. The scenes are grouped according to the type of relationship: dating, parenting, friends, work and a few universal situations. You can adapt the suggested responses to fit similar or parallel issues in your life.

The brief and compact information that follows represents a highly condensed compendium of the practical knowledge I've accumulated over the past years, as well as major ideas from my previous two books, *Emotional Bullshit* and *Beyond Blame*. The most fundamental message in both is to create greater success in all your relationships by eliminating blame from your communications. While those books traced the dynamics of moving past blame and offered some general advice, this book offers the exact words to avoid using two of its components—criticism and accusation.

There really *are* ways to express feelings and ask for what you need *effectively* without hurting other people, and without using blame.

Say This, Not That will quickly show you the way.

The Unique Purpose of This Book

There are a few lucky people who seem to be born with the natural skill for speaking well in just about any situation—no matter how demanding.

Then there's the rest of us.

I grew up with a severely critical father. He himself grew up in a harshly critical family in which praise or compliments were considered (at best) unnecessary and (at worst) guaranteed to "spoil" a child.

It took several years of therapy to learn that my family had conditioned my fight/flight response to instantly react to criticism or accusation. Even the slightest bit of either one would send my body temperature soaring. My face would flush, my throat tighten—I'd barely be able to speak—and all I'd want to do was run away and hide. Occasionally I'd fight back with my own verbal attack. Needless to say, these responses did not help me get along in the world.

Why was I so reactive? people would wonder. To me it seemed entirely normal, because my body did not know how to react any other way. My repertoire of responses was limited to one.

When I began my training as a therapist, I was blessed with the opportunity to work directly with Pia Mellody (author of *Facing Codependence* and other books). After several gut-wrenching workshops, I learned that what I had accepted as a fairly typical childhood had really been a systematic reign of terror in which ordinary childhood mistakes were severely punished, both emotionally and physically. There was virtually no space for even common childhood blunders. For instance, spilling a glass of milk was close to a capital crime.

During my first decade of practice, I delved deeply into the childhood history of my patients in an effort to help them recognize how their early training influenced their day-to-day interactions. It was very helpful for them to learn why they were so reactive. They wanted to know why they continued to make the same mistakes over and over, both in their relationships and at work.

Ultimately, however, it turned out that, more than anything, they needed help in how to behave in the present. "Okay, I know that I'm reactive," James or Kaitlin would say. "I know I need to stop making things worse. But what do I do—what can I say when . . . ?"

The unique purpose of *Say This, Not That* is to provide the answer to this core question. Along the way I'll discuss and clarify the THREE FACTORS that are vital to speaking effectively with others:

- *First*, communication involves **strategy**—that is, thoughtful planning about the best way to approach an issue. This book will help you develop a **strategically** effective plan for saying the right words at the right time.
- *Second*, effective communication involves **more than just words**. This book provides specific suggestions about the most effective body language, gestures and even (at times) silence to get your ideas across and precisely communicate what you want, feel or need in a wide variety of circumstances.
- *Third*, your **physical body** and range of **emotions influence** how you talk and the **words you actually say**. Even a moderate amount of physical excitement can overwhelm your ability to choose the right phrase or sentence. Learning how to step back and think calmly

before responding in challenging situations can make all the difference.

It is essential to have specific plans for what to say in situations in which you might be overwhelmed with emotion. It can be very dangerous if you don't know what to say. Or find that what you've already said isn't helping or is making matters worse. Better to be prepared.

———•————•———

All three of these factors are crucially important in a broad range of speaking situations.

Whether discussing a business issue with a coworker, dealing with a stressful question from your spouse or partner, holding a necessary conversation with your child or even having an exchange with a stranger on the street, it's vital to know which words will be most effective. To that end, you'll also need to know which part of your usual repertoire you need to relearn.

Again, whenever we're talking face-to-face with another person (or even *thinking* about a confrontation) it doesn't take much stress to trigger a negative reaction. Within a few milliseconds you can find yourself saying words you never *intended* to say, and all the more so when the other person is important to you.

For example, let's take Jane and Eduardo. When they walked into my consulting office, their stiff body language and tight expressions told me that they had probably just had a nasty argument. I asked them to tell me what had just happened. After some prompting, Eduardo gave me a hard look and said, "I love Jane . . . but she's a fanatic. She's a perfectionist. She doesn't have blood in her veins like normal people. Nothing I do is ever good enough. She's impossible to please. Just impossible!"

Whew.

Jane's face had become flushed. As might be expected, she responded in kind. "Well, I thought I was marrying a *man*, not a selfish adolescent who cares more about sports than anything else—including his *children*."

Ouch.

I took a deep breath and kept my facial expression neutral to let them know that their verbal barrage didn't upset me. I asked them to give me some history involving their relationship: how they had met, how long they'd been married, etc. I learned that they'd met in college, been married for ten years and had two children.

I next asked them to identify their *intention*: Why were they coming to see a therapist about their relationship? What were they hoping to achieve?

To my surprise, each one affirmed that despite a plethora of grievances, they wanted to stay together. While each occasionally threatened divorce, they really did not want to separate.

This was vital for me to know, since I would be asking them to do some difficult emotional work and make some changes in their habits. I needed to know if they were willing to do that work, or if one or both were already searching for an exit.

In fact, Jane and Eduardo were still devoted to each other. But their devotion was rapidly dissipating because they had been unable to stop spewing criticisms and accusations.

To make matters even worse, they had developed a dreadful repertoire of snorts, grunts, snarls, sarcastic chuckles, frowns, raised eyebrows and other ways of communicating disdain.

Their life together had, in short, become a daily hell.

———

Jane and Eduardo clearly needed a script to work from, because they were too emotionally exhausted and overwhelmed with resentment and anxiety to *think clearly* about what they really wanted to say. Criticizing each other had become a toxic habit. And that habit, the cycle of attack and defense and attack, had to be broken.

So I wrote them a script: specific words to say, and directions about how to say them, including pauses and inflections, instead of the destructive dialogue they were now employing.

Why such a detailed, specific approach? Because, to repeat, when we're overwhelmed with negative emotions, our ability to **think** is severely compromised. A prepared script avoids the need to think. In essence, it does the thinking for us.

And it worked. Having a written dialogue they could use during moments of emotional stress helped direct them toward more positive and loving messages.

And that's exactly what this book can do for you.

Why Using Scripts Can Make All the Difference

Of course, using a preorganized "formula" like a script in a particular situation can seem contrived and artificial. And it is—for several very *positive* reasons.

Referring to a script when you need to say something to another person is, above all, a method of learning. Namely, it's a way to learn the words that work—and the words that don't.

Learning a new skill is the key point.

Most important, the skills you learn are adaptable. Once you've trained your mind to think in scripts, you'll be able to carry over the concepts to other challenging situations.

NOTE: I want to emphasize this last point—the skill of learning a specific script can be adapted to every other situation in life. Learning the most effective way of stating your case, asking for something you need, or defending yourself from a verbal attack are skills that will serve you in every encounter.

———

The first script I taught Jane and Eduardo didn't even involve words. I diagnosed their problem as *too much communication*, almost all of it toxic. Each of them reacted either verbally or with body language to *every* comment, unable to let anything slide.

So their first set of instructions was to practice silence, combined with a neutral body posture and especially a neutral facial expression whenever they were together, and especially when one of them was feeling tense. These instructions may sound simple, but were extremely difficult for them. Both struggled mightily not to revert to old habits.

After learning to simply remain silent when things got tough, the next crucial behavior they needed to learn was to communicate without blame.

What they said to each other *had to* be free of both criticism and accusation, two of the principal components of blame.

So when Jane was upset with Eduardo about not turning off the TV and coming to dinner, instead of saying something sarcastic and derogatory, the scripts I provided trained her to say, *"It's important to me to share family time together during meals."* Notice that these words do not accuse or criticize, they simply *imply* that Jane wants Eduardo to join the other family members, and allow him to make his own decision.

This approach may seem very mild. But there's a solid psychological basis for this, which we'll discuss in greater depth in some of the sections dealing with difficult situations.

Not only does Jane now declare her wishes to Eduardo without criticizing, she has shifted the focus to what she needs and away from her anger and resentment.

After just a few days of each refraining from critical, accusatory, punishing, or humiliating comments, Jane and Eduardo noticed they were beginning to feel more positive toward each other. And that improvement in their home and family life has continued.

Please notice two things about their success. First, this approach worked for them because they both really wanted to find ways to stay together. Neither of them was seeking an exit. In short, the techniques I taught them matched their true intent. Positive intent is absolutely necessary to improve communication.

Second, as Jane and Eduardo learned to take better care in their communications with each other, they also learned far better ways to take care of *themselves*.

Which leads to an overriding concept intrinsic to this book:

Learning to communicate more effectively is an intrinsic part of self-care.

I'm defining self-care as *taking care of your long-term best interests* in the hundreds of small decisions that carry you toward—or away from—your goals.

The opposite of self-care is self-indulgence; giving in to any urge that satisfies a short-term impulse, without regard to the long-term consequences. When you criticize someone close to you because that's what you feel like doing in that moment, that's being self-indulgent.

So when you learn how to use new methods of communicating, you are also learning how to take care of your personal needs: in short, practicing self-care.

Now let's examine the five basic rules that will help you take care of yourself.

The Five Rules of Effective Communication

I call these concepts "rules" for two reasons: because breaking them has inevitable negative consequences, and learning them will pay tremendous dividends. There's a direct correlation between the number of rules you incorporate into your words and gestures and your level of satisfaction in relationships. Simply put, the more you follow these rules, the happier you will be. And the more successful you'll be in life.

Conversely, the less you use them, the more stressful, frustrated and resentful you'll be. And the less successful you'll be.

That's a basic fact.

THE FIVE RULES OF EFFECTIVE COMMUNICATION:

1. Decide in advance what you want to accomplish.
2. Say only what you need to say; nothing more.
3. Don't ask questions that don't have an actual answer.
4. Do not use blame: no criticism, accusation, punishment or humiliation.
5. Always be ready to stop when things get too heated.

RULE ONE ▶ Decide in advance what you want to accomplish.

The question of **intention**—what you want to accomplish—is one of the least explored areas of communication. Few of us take the time necessary to figure out what we *intend to accomplish* with a question or comment before launching in. Then we're amazed when an apparently simple remark ignites a firefight.

What, for example, does Daniel intend to accomplish when he looks over his son's fifth-grade homework and barks, "You call this homework? Do you think you can get away with this kind of sloppy work?" What is

Daniel's intention behind these comments? If he's out to teach his son responsibility, is this blast of criticism going to help?

In fact, Daniel believes that criticizing his son is an effective way to teach him responsibility. Sadly, he's operating under a *mistaken belief*. Namely, that using critical, accusatory and even humiliating language encourages diligence and hard work.

And if he continues to use such harsh language with his son, their relationship will suffer. If it suffers badly enough, the consequences can be severe.

So one of my most common suggestions to patients is to ask them to clarify the goals and long-term best interests behind even their simplest statements—*before* opening their mouths. To ask themselves: "What's my intention? What do I want to accomplish? What do I need from this person right now?"

Pausing to ask yourself what you want to accomplish takes effort and self-discipline. It also requires personal courage—the willingness to do something that's inherently difficult and even, at times, a bit frightening.

I can categorically state: *The few seconds that you take to examine your intention before you speak may be the most valuable few seconds of your entire day.*

RULE TWO ▶ Say only what you need to say—nothing more.

My experience with people speaking together had taught me that most people don't know how to stick to the point and say only what's needed—and nothing more. They don't know how to keep it simple. Or when to stop.

For example, let's return to Jane and Eduardo in the midst of a therapy session, after they'd been practicing with scripts for over a month.

I asked them about a recent "date" they'd scheduled, and whether Eduardo had had a good time with Jane. He hesitated before offering a conditional "Yes."

Had he thanked his wife for coming with him?

"Ah, no," Eduardo replied. "Am I supposed to?"

"If you want to encourage her to do so again, yes," I said. "Everyone likes to hear positive reactions for something they do."

He thought for a moment, then turned to his wife. "Uh, Jane, thanks for coming along the other night." He paused. "I had a good time. And I appreciate that you didn't bring your usual sour attitude."

As could be expected, Jane instantly grew tense.

"Whoa!" I ordered. "Eduardo, please rewind. After 'I had a good time'—just stop."

"But I'm just telling her that she wasn't—" he tried to argue.

"No, you're not," I said. "You're dumping a load of past resentments. You're sabotaging your progress. Unless that's your intention—to make matters worse—just say exactly what you mean. Nothing more."

Eduardo slowly nodded in recognition. It seemed he'd gotten the point.

The key to success is keeping your words right to the point. Don't add words that discount your message and sabotage the positive content of your communications.

RULE THREE ▶ Don't ask questions that don't have an actual answer.

Many people develop a style of speaking that asks a lot of "false questions." Also known as rhetorical questions, in real life they irritate the other person because they're not honest attempts to get information. Psychologically, the intention is to discharge anxiety and resentment, not to gather factual information.

Hidden inside false questions are negative messages, thinly veiled criticisms, or even direct attacks. The other person hears that, and resents it.

Here are some examples of false questions (delivered in an acidic tone of voice):

- "Why did you leave the mayonnaise out again?" Implied criticism: *You're too inconsiderate to put it away.*
- "Why don't you pay more attention when I talk to you?" Implied criticism: *You're too immature to actually listen.*
- "Why didn't you call your mother on her birthday?" Implication: *Because you're selfish, don't love your mother, don't care about anyone.*
- "Why are you tailgating that car? Why are you always in such a rush?" *Try to figure out the criticisms in these questions.*

Clearly, these false questions are not designed to collect factual information or build closeness and trust. What emotions do you feel when you read them? Probably frustration, resentment, maybe even rage. Many of the scripts in the book highlight false questions—interrogations that don't really request information but are actually designed to vent frustration, resentment, anxiety or other negative emotions and toss them at the other person. They are all examples of unhealthy and unhelpful communication.

RULE FOUR ▶ Do not use blame: No criticism, accusation, punishment or humiliation.

This rule is complex. In my previous book *Beyond Blame*, I spend 319 pages discussing the ravages of blame. The premise: Using blame is always destructive because it's actually made up of four toxic behaviors—*criticism, accusation, punishment and humiliation*—that only create anger, anxiety and distrust.

Not only do these behaviors do absolutely nothing to solve problems, but the negative emotions they set off *always* push people further away. Absolutely *no one* enjoys being the target of criticism, accusation, punishment or humiliation.

"But," you may ask, "if my boyfriend/spouse/child behaves badly, don't I have the right to tell him? When my feelings are hurt, if I don't criticize him, how can I get him to change?"

These questions are valid and deserve answers, some of which this book presents briefly in the following scenes. For a more in-depth discussion about how blame functions negatively in all our lives, please refer to *Beyond Blame*.

For now, I'll simply state that you can accomplish these goals without resorting to any of the four negative behaviors involved in blame. And the scripts will show you how.

RULE FIVE ➤ Always be ready to stop when things get too heated.

You must be willing to step away from a discussion if it starts to become too heated.

Anytime you feel yourself starting to become overwhelmed with either information or feelings, you need to be able to stop. It doesn't matter whether the conversation involves a minor discussion about breakfast or a major debate about selling the house.

The mechanism for stopping a conversation that's becoming overheated is extremely simple. It can be contained in a one-sentence agreement both parties accept. Here it is:

Either party can ask to stop a discussion at any time for any reason.

What that means is that whenever you ask to stop talking about something, the other person is obligated to stop talking and give a simple "Okay." No further discussion occurs, not even "I just need to finish my thought" or "Why can't I just explain . . . ?"

When I suggest this idea to argumentative couples, their typical reply is, "Oh, great. My spouse will shut me up all the time. I'll never be able to talk about anything that matters to me."

In actual practice, though, that rarely happens. Even the most out-of-control couples have demonstrated that when the people involved have in place a solid agreement to stop talking, both people benefit. That's because when either person can ask to stop talking when he or she feels overwhelmed, and finds that request respected, each person can begin to trust—often for the first time in years—that bringing up a potentially difficult topic will not automatically escalate into all-out verbal warfare.

Of course, the above assumes that the basic **intention** of all involved is to improve the relationship. If any party harbors the intention to sabotage the relationship or to gain control, then no mechanism can help. But again, several decades of therapeutic experience have taught me that that's rarely the case.

These Five Rules of Effective Communication (see page 14) will show up throughout this book, and we'll explore variations of them in a number of the scripts.

How to Use the Scripts in Real Life

Finally, let's take a quick look at how to actually use the following scripts in real-life situations.

When looking over the scripts, some readers might complain: *It's not natural to talk this way. I need to say what's on my mind, to be myself.*

And that's true. But you need to be your *best* self. The most skilled self you can be. People are complex. Relationships can be difficult. And how well you learn to navigate those difficulties will determine how successful you'll be.

One more essential point: Highly successful people *do* follow scripts. People who flourish in their relationships and especially in their careers talk in simple, direct sentences that don't rankle, confuse, irritate or offend other people. They speak economically, saying just what's needed and nothing more. Their scripts seem to be part of their internal communication structure. If you watch or listen to people who have been in public life for decades and are widely respected for their views and careers, you will notice that they speak this way naturally.

———•———

As you leaf through the scripts, start with the version on the left page— the DON'T SAY THIS section—and then look over the SAY THIS page to the right. Go back and forth a few times. Study how different the approaches are.

Then apply each pair of pages to yourself. How do the two sections line up with your own ways of speaking? Are they similar to situations that arise in your own life and relationships?

Do you use the sorts of words on the DON'T SAY THIS pages? If so, what kind of reactions have they provoked?

On the SAY THIS pages, do parts of the suggested phrases strike home? Are there parts that you find yourself remembering? Or that you might want to memorize?

Once you see how you can use the scripts as a set of crib sheets, a way to review your "homework" to see where you made errors, it's easy to figure out what to do to improve your future performance. And, yes, verbal communication—speaking to another person out loud—*is* a series of actions, a complex carrying-out of an intention, a performance.

———•———

As you think over all these things, notice the primary theme encompassed in all the scripts: THOUGHTFULNESS.

Keeping all this in mind, especially the Five Rules of Effective Communication, requires quite a bit of *thinking*. Once you're willing to think about what you're saying, thoughtfulness will help you act in your best interests.

The more you analyze the meaning of the words you intend to speak, practice your lines and rehearse your best delivery, the more mastery of communication you'll bring to your relationships.

I recall many years ago working on a project with a young man who was only in his early twenties but was already gifted with a natural talent for communication. Whenever I found it necessary to say something critical to him, he'd nod, his face the picture of receptivity and interest. Then he'd say something either neutral or disarming, such as "Yeah, I sometimes forget that." I would always leave the encounter feeling very positive about what had just happened—no matter how intense or potentially difficult the situation.

What impressed me most was his effortless skill.

Then again, there's the rest of us—who have to study and struggle with our communication problems, typically lamenting how difficult the *other person* is.

It's my hope that these pages will help end those laments and put you on the path of learning the skills of effective communication—one script, and one conversation, at a time.

So let's begin with what people say to each other when they first meet, that torturous process called *dating*. That's when the two people involved have their antennae operating at full capacity and the slightest error can be wildly misinterpreted.

PART ONE

Dating: What to Say— and What Not to Say

Dating: It's all about anxiety.

After all, your entire future may depend on the next few minutes.

If you make a really good impression on the person you're meeting for the first time on an actual date, if the person thinks you're cute and clever and sincere and sexy and he/she might want to keep on seeing you and (eventually) have sex and . . . somewhere in there, you might even fall in love.

Falling in love (assuming the dating goes well) is also filled with anxiety. When you give your heart to another person, you give the most precious part of yourself. Nothing causes anxiety as much as possible heartbreak.

And if you fall in love, you might also commit your future to that person. And your sweetheart might not imagine the future as you do.

In short, a lot is at stake during that first date. So it makes sense that you will want to avoid saying things that might jeopardize either your future or your heart.

●——————●

Dating is an area of human interaction in which the Five Rules of Effective Communication need to be modified and reduced to fit the demands of this complex human activity. I call them the Four Guidelines for Talking to Your Date.

These guidelines address the most common mistakes people make when they meet someone for the first (or second or third) time with the intention of possibly beginning (or continuing) a romantic relationship.

IMPORTANT NOTE: The following scripts are designed to help you learn new skills and behaviors, not to help you be *false* or *manipulative*. We're talking about skills—not about faking it. *These are behaviors to learn, not a personality to adopt.* They engage your thinking, rather than your anxiety, so you can make the best choices. And, paradoxically, the more you know about how to choose the best words and communicate the most effectively, the more you'll be able to express your most authentic self.

To that end, note the following:

FOUR GUIDELINES FOR TALKING TO YOUR DATE

1. Maintain positive or neutral nonverbal gestures and expressions.
2. Don't ask invasive, demanding or judgmental questions.
3. Don't be vague about your intentions; explicitly and strategically state your needs.
4. Follow your instincts and always be ready to leave if things get too uncomfortable.

Let's quickly review each guideline to see how it applies to meeting with someone new.

GUIDELINE ONE ▶ Maintain positive or neutral nonverbal gestures or expressions.

Well, of course! you might say. *I'm not going to scowl or be unfriendly.* But it's not easy to be aware of your facial expressions, body posture and the many gestures that constitute a large part of what you're trying to express.

At least half of all communication during dating is nonverbal.

In fact, your facial expressions, posture, gestures and overall physical bearing are probably more important than the words you say. I recall a female patient named Sandra who complained about the last few men she'd dated. One had stared at her chest so often that she felt like an object being scrutinized. Another kept glancing nervously around the room. Another repeatedly answered his cell phone. Sandra reported these behaviors as having a chilling effect on her desire to date any of these men ever again.

GUIDELINE TWO ▶ Don't ask invasive, demanding or judgmental questions.

Once again this may sound obvious. Yet you'd be surprised at how often people quickly ask a question that's highly personal, or is tinged with judgment and criticism.

Sandra described her first date with Bruce. She wanted to know whether Bruce was in a relationship, or even married, so she asked him directly: "So, Bruce, I assume you're not married or living with someone . . . I mean, you're not just interested in having an affair?" Well, that question, coupled with Sandra's tight-lipped expression, really put him off.

Asking someone directly whether he is married or in a relationship is not inherently wrong. But then to virtually accuse someone of being the kind of man who's "just interested in having an affair" is not only judgmental, but hints at a suspicious, perhaps even paranoid, personality.

Bruce wasn't very skilled at asking questions, either. When he asked Sandra about her job as a legal secretary he blurted out, "Have you considered becoming an attorney . . . or is it enough for you to just be a secretary?"

Ouch! Sandra was proud of her job and recoiled at hearing his implied criticism. She worked for two attorneys and considered herself an indispensable part of the overall legal team. How dare he demean her professional status!

It may be that in your previous dates you've asked questions that were overly invasive or innately critical. The scripts that follow can help you soften up your delivery.

GUIDELINE THREE ▶ Don't be vague about your intentions; explicitly and strategically state your needs.

This guideline requires quite a bit of sensitivity. You don't want to blurt out that you're looking for the mother—or the father—of your children! At the same time, you don't want to spend months (or even years) trying to convince another person to fulfill a need or wish (such as having children) that the other person has no intention of fulfilling.

If establishing a lifelong relationship is one of your needs, you have to be as clear about that as soon as you can. If, however, the person you're dating is only into partying and having fun, and monogamy is not on his or her mind, then you also need to find that out relatively soon.

One effective way to get a lot of basic information about the other person is to find out what your date likes to do for fun and recreation. Deidre learned, for example, that Reggie played golf and tennis whenever possible, and took trips to go diving in the summer and skiing during the winter. Did he have time for a relationship? Sure, as long as his girlfriend came along and either played with him or watched him play. Because Deidre wasn't much into sports, she figured out quickly and painlessly that they weren't a good match.

Which was a good thing, because it's a waste of your time to date someone whose needs and intentions are too divergent from yours.

GUIDELINE FOUR ➡ Follow your instincts, and always be ready to leave if things get too uncomfortable.

Roberto has been dating Veronica for three months. They get along well, the sex is fantastic, but Roberto is increasingly worried about Veronica's tendency to get angry very quickly when anything goes wrong. Last night he knocked over a glass of water and she called him clumsy. She later apologized, but then, when he made a wrong turn while driving, she snorted at him derisively. Now he gets nervous when he's around her.

And he's wise to feel anxious. We often overlook serious warning flags that indicate a submerged problem that will become only more volatile as time goes on. In Roberto's case, as he realizes that he's feeling tension in Veronica's presence, he needs to follow his instincts and tell her that the relationship isn't working for him.

Now let's get into the actual scripts and see how these four guidelines apply in each of them.

What a Cutie!

THE SITUATION: *You see someone in the café you frequent whom you've noticed a few times before. Your heart races. You'd really like to go out on a date with this person and you don't know if you'll have the opportunity to run into him or her again. You're nervous; what should you say?*

DON'T SAY THIS: *"I just wanted to tell you that you're really cute. Do you want to go out?"*

MISTAKE: Too direct and intimidating. (Sending the wrong message: I'm pushy and blunt.) A too-direct approach might embarrass the person into refusing, even though he or she might really want to accept.

HOW MIGHT THE PERSON RESPOND? Most likely the cutie's pulse will race—but probably not out of pleasure. Being confronted so directly is intimidating. Expect an RR, a Reactive Response. Almost certainly the person will feel too much emotion to think clearly, and you'll probably hear some version of "Get lost."

WHAT'S A REACTIVE RESPONSE? When something triggers the fight/flight syndrome hardwired into our nervous systems. When we feel physically or emotionally threatened, stress shoots adrenaline into our blood, and we're ready for action, not for thinking. So your overly aggressive approach will likely get a response of either fight or flight—not a date.

REALITY CHECK: Research shows that people of both genders appreciate attention if delivered tactfully and respectfully. A courteous invitation, even from a stranger, can be a delight. You don't have to be super-suave; a heartfelt request complete with stutters and false starts can signal sincerity. You might get a smile and a polite refusal, but you most probably won't get a fight or a flight.

SAY THIS: *"Excuse me if I'm interrupting, but I've noticed you here a few times and I wonder if you've got time to have coffee with me."* (Sending the right message: I'm courteous and honest in my approach.)

AND REMEMBER: Take a minute to make sure the person is alone. At all times maintain eye contact and smile or maintain a pleasant expression.

BE AWARE: Since a majority of people are already in relationships and therefore not available, your chances of hearing a "yes" are less than half. So be ready for rejection.

POSSIBLE RESPONSES: The person might not be available so he or she might say, "I'm sorry, but I can't." To which you respond, "Oh, I'm sorry to hear that. Well, thank you anyway." Then walk away and get on with your life. If you're really lucky you might hear, "Thank you. I'd like that."

KEEP IN MIND THOSE OLD WORDS OF WISDOM: Nothing ventured, nothing gained. If you don't take risks, you won't move ahead. Also remind yourself that all you're doing is talking to a stranger in a public setting. The risk to your personal safety is around zero. If you don't take the risk of approaching someone you find attractive, it's virtually 100 percent certain that you won't get to know that person. You risk not beginning a new and wonderful relationship.

Whoa! She's Interested!

THE SITUATION: *A woman you don't know very well from your hiking club asks you for a date and you want to accept. How should you handle it?*

DON'T SAY THIS: *"Well, I don't have anything better to do"* or *"Guess it's a way to kill time"* or *"Yeah, I think I can spare a couple of hours."*

AND DEFINITELY DON'T SAY THIS: *"Sure, your place or mine?"* or *"Best offer I've had all day."* (Sending the wrong message: My attempts at humor show a deeper insecurity.)

NEVER USE SARCASM: Or any kind of tasteless humor that could sabotage your true intention. You may never get another chance to make that good first impression.

NERVOUSNESS IS NORMAL: If you're embarrassed or nervous at receiving a direct invitation, you *yourself* may experience a Reactive Response. Your symptoms—increased heart rate, flushed face, sweating—may provoke you to say something flip or silly that's contrary to what you really mean or *want*. Remember: Just as it can be nerve-racking for you to approach someone you don't know very well, it's likely going to be just as difficult for the person approaching *you*. Be gentle in your response.

TAKE YOUR TIME: It's perfectly okay to ask for a minute to think about the request. Slow down and spend a few seconds to think about the response that best fits your needs and desires. A time-out slows down the surge of adrenaline that accompanies fear or excitement and prevents it from too strongly influencing your reply. It allows your thinking process to return.

SAY THIS: *"Thank you. Yes, I'd like to have coffee with you."* With a smile. (Sending the right message: I'm able to make an adult decision, gracefully.)

REALITY CHECK: All you're agreeing to is having coffee in a public place, a neutral territory in the company of others. You're mature enough to control your destiny, and can stop the progress of the relationship at any time if you need to. You're consenting to coffee, not a marriage proposal.

TRUST YOUR INTUITION: One of the most common fears related to accepting that first "date" is that the other person might have a hidden history and might be troublesome or even dangerous. Obviously, if your intuition is sending signals that appear as chills down your spine, then you need to heed your instincts and say no or otherwise exit the conversation.

IF IT STARTS GETTING ODD: If after you accept and the other person tries to set up an odd time or place to meet, or acts in any way that bothers you, it's absolutely okay to say: "Sorry, I've changed my mind about having coffee." Extracting yourself from a date will likely feel *very* uncomfortable, but it's much better than ignoring warning signs and allowing yourself to be drawn into a bad situation.

Not Really Into It

THE SITUATION: *A colleague from another department at your company asks you for a date—and you don't find this person interesting or attractive. How do you politely but effectively say no?*

DON'T SAY: *"Well, I'm really busy these days. I . . . uh, I'm taking care of my sick mother."*

DON'T GIVE A PHONY OR OVERSTATED EXCUSE. Offering false information extends the discomfort for both people and puts you in a bad light. (Sending the wrong message: I'm insecure and nervous.)

BE KIND BUT TRUTHFUL: Over the years I've accumulated information from patients of all ages about how they respond in dating situations. The consensus is that elaborate or phony-sounding excuses don't work for anyone. People want to hear words that are direct, honest and clearly stated. Admittedly, practicing straight talk might be more difficult and provoke more anxiety, but a clear and direct message is the most effective.

REALITY CHECK: There's no way to totally eliminate the anxiety involved in either directly asking someone you don't know well for a date—or being asked. In the old days, a third person such as a relative or matchmaker would do that job. Today some Internet services play the role of matchmaker. But the nature of dealing with relative strangers has not changed. Dating anxiety is an inevitable part of social life.

SAY THIS: *"Thank you, but I'm not available for dating."* This reply is the minimum necessary. It directly describes your situation. (Sending the right message: I know what I want.)

HONESTY CHECK: If you do not find the person interesting or attractive, then, indeed, you are *not* available. That is, *emotionally* available. Saying you're not is therefore an honest response.

SAYING NO IS TOUGH: In our culture, it seems to be more difficult for women to directly say no. But these situations are awkward and difficult for any gender. Giving evasive excuses or long-winded explanations only makes the situation more difficult for everyone. Say what you need to say, then stop.

BUT DIRECT IS BEST: Being honest, direct and succinct is a major skill in communicating effectively. Even when talking with a complete stranger, you have a chance to engage in a positive exchange. The most important rule is to never (needlessly) offend anyone. Every script in *Say This, Not That* directs you toward staying positive—because that's what successful communicators do.

REMAIN FIRM: In case the other person asks more questions or tries to insist, stick to your initial refusal.

SAY THIS: *"I already explained that I'm not available to date. Please accept my refusal. Thank you."* Saying these words firmly, with a neutral facial expression and posture, should be enough.

Uh-oh . . . I Have to Describe Myself . . .

THE SITUATION: *You want to join a dating group, event or Internet site. What words do you use to describe yourself?*

DON'T SAY THIS: *"I'm a wonderful person with a great sense of humor who likes people of all kinds, and who loves movies, candlelit dinners, long walks and good conversation."* (Sending the wrong message: I like everything indiscriminately.)

SKIP GLOWING GENERIC DESCRIPTIONS: Focusing only on positive romantic activities that pretty much everyone enjoys makes you sound superficial and less than self-aware. Popular romance movies may feature love-struck couples enjoying candlelit dinners, taking long walks and engaging in intimate conversations, but that's the fantasy part of romance. Real life is much more complicated. Attracting a potential date requires more than generic homilies about oneself; it demands honesty and direct communication right up front.

AVOID EXCESSIVE ADJECTIVES: Avoid terms that sound too good to be true, even if they might be. Examples: *handsome, studly, masculine, muscular, sexy, beautiful, foxy, svelte,* etc. Heaps of self-praise, such as "I'm lots of fun" or "My friends say I'm a real catch" aren't really convincing. "I'm waiting to be discovered" sounds more like an invitation to solve a creepy mystery than a pleasant time.

SAY THIS: Write a list of your most positive characteristics, then another list of your less than wonderful traits. If you love to play all kinds of sports, you might add that sometimes you neglect your other responsibilities. If you're dedicated to your job, also note if it's sometimes tough for you to take time off. If you're very social and love people and parties, also mention that you occasionally skip vacuuming your apartment. (Sending the right message: I'm self-aware and authentic.)

BOILING IT DOWN: Provide a candid self-assessment. Everyone has positive and negative traits. *Everyone.* Emphasizing both makes you come across as self-aware and self-accepting.

ALWAYS AIM FOR HONESTY: We know that "honesty" is subject to interpretation—especially in dating. But if you start with a sincere effort to present a realistic version of yourself, you'll be far ahead of the game.

REAL-LIFE STORY: Mikel had tried online dating several times but was always disappointed. A close friend offered to help him with both his profile and how he responded to those showing interest. After a lot of effort, Mikel presented a far more balanced view of himself that strongly appealed to women who were tired of men who used inflated descriptions about themselves but were disappointing in person. Eventually, telling the more complete truth won Mikel someone who proved to be a solid and deeply lovable person.

My Date Is Wonderful! ·

THE SITUATION: *You're on your first date and your heart is fluttering. You like the other person a lot! What do you say?*

DON'T SAY THIS: *"You're absolutely fantastic. I think we've got a great future!"* or *"It feels like destiny has brought us together."* (Sending the wrong message: I'm over the top with drama.)

MISTAKE: Far too theatrical and intimidating. Perhaps worse, it's corny.

HOW MIGHT THE PERSON RESPOND? Asserting that there *must* be a future between the two of you is likely to scare off your date, who might fear that this is the start of an obsession or stalking situation. Citing fate or destiny to predict the future of your relationship is likely to elicit a RR, a Reactive Response, and the other person may be overwhelmed.

PACE, DON'T PUSH: Pacing is everything. Allowing the relationship to develop naturally is the healthiest and most effective strategy. No one likes being pushed, especially when it comes to meeting a new person and (possibly) beginning a romance.

REAL-LIFE STORY: Bryan was immediately smitten when he met Alice. She also liked him, and they arranged to go out for dinner. Bryan believed he had finally met his soul mate. The next day, he bought two dozen red roses, wrote a long passionate poem, invited her on a weeklong cruise, and left everything outside her door. Alice was so overwhelmed by Bryan's excessive enthusiasm that she refused to return his calls. Bryan was crushed. "How could Alice not see that we're soul mates?"

SAY THIS: *"I'd really like to see you again. Would you like to get together?"* (Sending the right message: I know how to pace myself.)

KEEP IT SIMPLE: Asking a direct, simple question allows space for the other person to make a decision without undue pressure. Not only is it respectful, but psychologically it's also the healthiest way to proceed.

REAL-LIFE STORY: Mirabel thought Sal was a nice guy but worried about his emotional availability, given that he had two small children who spent half their time with him. For his part, Sal thought that Mirabel was utterly fantastic, so when it took Mirabel a day or two to return his calls, he didn't pressure her. For her part, Mirabel needed time to think about getting involved with a guy who had children, and appreciated the lack of pressure. She also liked that he didn't immediately give up if she didn't respond instantly. Sal's patience paid off, and after a few weeks, they started seeing each other regularly.

APPLY ANCIENT WISDOM: Several wise sayings apply here: Patience is key. Perseverance furthers. One day at a time. Don't cross a bridge until you come to it. Sal was actually "courting" Mirabel and needed to be skillful in his approach. Fortunately, he was mature enough to know that his children could be a little scary for a new person to deal with, so he took his time and allowed Mirabel to set the pace. And that approach succeeded.

He Just Disappeared!

THE SITUATION: *You really like Sam and he seems to like you. After several fun dates, he stops calling and doesn't return your calls. What do you do?*

DON'T SAY THIS: Wait outside his workplace and confront him as he comes out: *"Why haven't you returned my calls? I thought you were a nice guy, but you're a jerk!"* (Sending the wrong message: I'm emotionally unstable . . . and scary.)

AGGRESSION IS INAPPROPRIATE: Belligerently confronting Sam is out of line, but a surprising proportion of people believe it would be justified. After all, hadn't you been dreaming of a blissful future with him? How dare he crush your dreams! Shouldn't he suffer the consequences of "deliberately" hurting you?

REVENGE IS NOT SWEET: The answers are no and no. Escalation is rarely a wise choice. Aggressively confronting Sam is playing "emotional vigilante." It creates a major incident that now becomes part of your personal history. Forever onward you'll be remembered as the person who made a scene at Sam's workplace. Do you want to be thought of as an emotional time bomb?

SAY THIS: E-mail or text him a simple note—*"I'm disappointed that I haven't heard from you."* That's all. (Sending the right message: I don't overreact when frustrated.)

ACT LIKE AN ADULT: While it's tempting to tell him he's a first-class jerk, your challenge is to *not* respond like an adolescent bent on revenge. You're a mature adult, so act like one. Sam has clearly lost interest and doesn't have the necessary emotional courage to tell you directly. That's his problem. Don't make it yours too by responding in kind.

LOOK IN THE MIRROR: What do *you* say to someone when you've lost interest? Do you do the right thing, which is tell people face-to-face that you want to discontinue the relationship? Call and talk directly to the person? Or at least leave a considerate message: "I'm sorry, but I have to tell you that it's not working for me and I don't want to continue seeing you. I hate to hurt your feelings this way, but I wanted you to know." If you do, count your good fortune in having achieved a high level of maturity. If not, don't get too annoyed when someone else shuts you out.

A FACT OF LIFE AND RELATIONSHIPS: Whenever you begin dating, you inherently accept an ethical obligation to act like an adult and clearly communicate your intentions. What the other person does or doesn't do is not within your control.

I'd Like to Know More

THE SITUATION: *Your friends Mark and Sarah have invited you to have dinner with their single friend Zeke. By the end of the dinner, despite some awkward moments, you like Zeke, and want to know more about him.*

DON'T (EITHER OF YOU) SAY THIS: *"I'm going on a wine-tasting trip next Saturday and Sunday—would you like to go along?"* (Sending the wrong message: I move quickly.)

WHAT'S THE PROBLEM? Such an invitation commits you to two whole days alone with someone you don't really know. The trip might easily degenerate into disaster. Even if you and Zeke turn out to be compatible, overloading your emotional circuits with so many demands so early on might jeopardize what could have been a solid relationship—if it had proceeded slowly. Allow things to develop at a gentle pace.

TAKE YOUR TIME: Even though popular culture is awash in romantic stories— love at first sight and flowering fondness blossoming into blissful romance within days (and then, of course, a beautiful wedding and living happily ever after)—reality is much more ordinary. It'll take time to figure out, for example, whether Zeke's shy awkwardness and distracted flightiness are deep structural parts of his personality, or just oddball reactions to meeting you. Similarly, he needs to know if your peculiarities run deep or are just momentary anomalies.

SAY THIS: *"Maybe we could get together and take a walk sometime. How does that sound?"* (Sending the right message: I know how to pace things.)

ONE STEP AT A TIME: Taking things slowly is always the most prudent course in life. This is never more critical than when you are just starting to date someone new.

HOLDING BACK THE HORMONAL RUSH: Up to eight different hormones can kick in—and quickly take over—when emotional juices flow fast and furious. Ever heard the morning-after lament: "What was I thinking!?" That's because, many times, you weren't. Nature has designed our bodies to react strongly when romantically inspired. After all, nature's goal is procreation: the making of babies. Romance reigns supreme as the primordial baby-making energy. Your brain doesn't have a chance against this flood. So holding back the hormonal rush is critical to avoiding a potentially life-distorting mistake.

HEALTHY BOUNDARIES ARE ESSENTIAL: Psychological boundaries protect you from the feelings, desires, needs and demands of other people—and your own. Being able to protect yourself from strong irrational influences—including attempts to get too close too fast—is a critical part of successful dating. For more on boundaries, see the "Boundaries" segment in the "Advanced Work" section at the end of this book.

Want to Spend the Night?

THE SITUATION: *You've just started dating—and really want to have sex.*

DON'T SAY THIS: *"You're really hot. I want to spend the night with you!"* (Sending the wrong message: Sex is more important than getting to know you.)

MISTAKE: Too fast and too pushy. Slow down! Newly dating couples (especially men) often feel pressure to move quickly into sex before either person knows much about the other. They're running on hormones and a host of other neuro-chemicals that get them excited.

RUSHING SEX CAN RUIN IT: This kind of "premature" invitation to have sex can produce tension and anxiety—which negatively affects sexual performance and the level of pleasure in both sexes.

NO SEX BEFORE ITS TIME: Even with today's easy access to factual information, people of both genders harbor mistaken beliefs about sex and sexual performance. These beliefs work against developing a healthy relationship.

SOME BAD BELIEFS: A lot of men believe that if they don't push to have sex right away, their date will consider them less masculine. Some women imagine that if their date hasn't asked for sex by the third date, he's probably gay. Many women also believe that they have to "capture" a guy with sex right away or he'll think they're "frigid" and might move on to "easier" women. These and many more mistaken beliefs about sex and gender roles can add stress to the early stages of a relationship.

SAY THIS: *"I find you very attractive . . . and I really look forward to a deeper relationship."* (Sending the right message: I'm interested in more than just sex.)

TIMING IS EVERYTHING: During the first few dates, when each party is carefully evaluating the other, it's wise to show that you're aware of the other person's needs. Not pushing into areas that may create stress shows that you're also able to act moderately; that you can be trusted. Trust is always the foundation of a good relationship.

WHAT'S YOUR PLAN? It's important to be clear on whether you see your date as someone you'd like to get to know better, someone with whom to develop a long-term relationship, or someone who's a sexual partner for a few encounters. In either case, be honest . . . with yourself and with your date! Using the First Rule of Communication—*decide what you want to accomplish*—can help you say the right thing at the right time to help nudge you toward your goal.

ADVANCED TIP: Remember that getting sexual with another person is one of the most intimate situations possible, and also the riskiest—emotionally and physically. Both people involved will be at their most vulnerable. Being thoughtful in what you say when *approaching, initiating, during and after sex* can avoid a lot of hurt feelings. It can also help build trust. And, as time goes on, help make intimacy more relaxed and loving.

I Was Dazzled by Love

THE SITUATION: *Rajiv is so smitten with Robin's lively personality, and their great sex, that he ignores her excessive drinking.*

DON'T SAY THIS *(to yourself)*: "Tomorrow will take care of itself." (Sending the wrong message: I'm irresponsible about my future.)

THE REAL ISSUE: This situation represents a serious issue in dating: ignoring a huge, flashing warning sign in the middle of the road. The fact that Robin starts out every date with a martini, drinks most of a bottle of wine and then wants a few more drinks when they're at Rajiv's apartment is a sign that something's very wrong. At first, Rajiv tells himself that Robin is only celebrating their great relationship . . . and fabulous sex.

DENIAL AT WORK: Rajiv simply refuses to see what's in front of his eyes, or minimizes its seriousness. This example illustrates how a person can live in "denial."

DON'T DELAY CONFRONTATION: When Rajiv eventually—after several months— tries to talk to Robin about her drinking, she ridicules him as a "lightweight" and finally calls him a "control freak." Rajiv, still entranced with her, backs off. Her drinking continues, and he decides that he may as well join her. Now every date with Robin gives him a bad hangover and lost time at work.

SAY THIS: *"I'm worried that every time we get together you have to drink. I'd like to have fun without the need for so much alcohol."* (Sending the right message: I'm capable of taking care of my basic needs.)

PUSHBACK: When Rajiv finally speaks up, Robin reacts vindictively. She becomes too "busy" to see Rajiv, hints at dating other men and leaves him messages about how other guys would love to have sex with her.

CONSULT WITH EXPERTS: Fortunately, rather than becoming depressed or giving in to Robin's threats, Rajiv consults a professional therapist. He learns about alcoholism and recalls that Robin has described several family members as being "drunks." The test of serious alcoholism? Whether the drinker insists on having several drinks at every social occasion—and criticizes anyone who comments.

STOP THE RELATIONSHIP IF NECESSARY: Rajiv tries several more times to spend time with Robin and restrict the drinking, but always fails. Their last two dates end up with her screaming. Rajiv finally decides to stop seeing Robin altogether. He's profoundly agitated and unhappy, but after a few weeks begins to be his old self, having learned an important lesson: You need to set your boundaries around drinking (or any worrisome behavior) early in the relationship.

I Thought Money Didn't Matter

THE SITUATION: *Deborah loves Mindy's artistic flair and easygoing ways. So she invites Mindy to share her loft, even though Mindy doesn't make a lot of money.*

DON'T SAY THIS *(to yourself)*: "Love's more important than money; I'll take care of our financial needs." (Sending the wrong message: I have no limits or boundaries.)

THE FANTASY OF TRUE LOVE: The fact that Mindy doesn't have a set work schedule allows her to take a walk or sit around and talk at any time. Deborah has never been with anyone so emotionally available. Mindy is always waiting for her no matter how late she works. And Mindy never complains.

COMPLICATIONS ARISE: After a few months Deborah realizes that the reason Mindy is so available is because, in fact, she doesn't work at all. Her art projects languish and her customers for graphic design have disappeared. Mindy has become entirely dependent on Deborah for financial support. Not only that, Mindy also has several siblings to whom she keeps on "lending" money "borrowed" from Deborah's account.

UNHAPPINESS GROWS: Deborah finds herself becoming snippy and sarcastic with Mindy, and finds the closeness and love she once felt giving way to resentment. Arguments boil to the surface, and occasionally they end in shouting matches filled with mutual accusations.

SAY THIS: *"I need balance in our relationship—I don't want to be the only one providing income."* (Sending the right message: I know how to take care of my long-term interests.)

THE NEED FOR LIMITS: If a relationship is going to be happy and fulfilling at any time in its development, the partners must reach an equitable agreement about shared responsibilities. Many new couples overlook these issues in the glow of their initial romance. But after they spend some time together, discrepancies in financial and other contributions become evident and cause frustration and even anger.

SETTING LIMITS AND STICKING TO THEM: When Deborah is certain that she feels exploited, she finally summons up the courage to sit down with Mindy and calmly tell her what she needs. Until they met Mindy had supported herself, although modestly, so Deborah insists that Mindy take on enough work to pay half of common expenses. And if Mindy refuses, Deborah tells her, they need to live separately.

SENDING A CLEAR SIGNAL: Mindy procrastinates for weeks until Deborah actually asks her to move. Finally Mindy gets it. She returns to focusing on her work and paying her way, and their relationship stabilizes.

Next we'll explore the complex issues that inevitably arise when two people have moved past dating and decided to mutually commit. Now the tough work really begins.

PART TWO

Developing a Long-Term Relationship

Developing a long-term successful relationship is all about perseverance. To persevere you must control your anxiety, restrain your impulses, not insist on being right at any cost—and keep on going.

Success in every relationship (coupling, parenting, friendship, work) requires the ability to control your anxiety and not give up. Because anxiety is a structural part of every human interaction, the closer the relationship, the greater the potential for anxiety. You must keep pushing yourself to learn new and effective ways of doing and saying things that bring you closer to your goal of happiness. To behave in ways you may have never considered before.

Fulfilling relationships require one more quality: moderation. This means that you don't overreact with a lot of furious and self-important energy. Nor do you act like a doormat, passively accepting disrespectful or irresponsible behavior.

The constant goal is to respond in a firm yet reasonable and moderate way.

Let me be clear: I believe that establishing fulfilling long-term relationships is one of our greatest achievements as human beings. Nature has designed us to live in families and groups—and living together as committed couples is part of this design. People who are married or in a relationship similar to marriage are, statistically, happier and healthier—and live longer.

Yet achieving success in committed long-term relationships remains, for most of us, our greatest challenge.

What you say—and don't say—goes a long way toward assuring either success or failure. A few well-chosen words, a kind gesture, even a smile delivered at the right moment can mean the difference between a nasty argument that wounds . . . or a reasonable discussion that promotes closeness and trust.

The following scripts focus on the challenges found in the early stages—during the first year or two—as well as the problems encountered in the more mature relationship that has weathered the early crises. Many issues, however, can apply to both stages.

But before we get started on the actual scripts, let's review some basic concepts at the heart of all successful relationships.

Research into why some couples are happy and others aren't has demonstrated that there are broad variations on how each couple defines happiness.

For instance, Kevin and Molly might talk to each other in volatile voices that would intimidate others, but they report high levels of satisfaction with each other. Sid and Rosine may discuss issues using oblique terms and semi-sentences that could appear vague and inconclusive, but that works for them. Both couples declare that they're quite happy with each other. Different methods and styles of communication may appear in your own life. (For more information, refer to John Gottman's *Seven Principles for Making Marriage Work*.)

There are, however, some basic rules and concepts that inform all styles. Namely, the Five Rules of Effective Communication, which we'll repeat here:

1. Decide in advance what you want to accomplish.
2. Say only what you need to say; nothing more.
3. Don't ask questions that don't have an actual answer.
4. Do not use blame: no criticism, accusation, punishment or humiliation.
5. Always be ready to stop when things get too heated.

These five rules are interwoven into all of the following scripts, which follow the progression of a relationship, beginning with issues that couples might encounter once they realize that they're committed to each other—the point at which each sees the other as a possible lifelong partner—and want to deepen that commitment.

Let's begin by using a script as a model, taking it apart phrase by phrase, and seeing how the five basic rules apply.

THE SITUATION: *You just moved in with Jude. His sports equipment is scattered everywhere. He'd said he'd organize it but still hasn't. You feel frustrated and disrespected.*

DON'T SAY THIS: *"Dammit, Jude, you promised you'd clean up this mess. Now keep your promise!"*

Let's look at this overall communication from the point of the Five Rules of Effective Communication.

RULE ONE ▶ Decide in advance what you want to accomplish.

What you want to accomplish is reasonable orderliness and space for yourself. That's the immediate goal. Beyond that, you also want to build a closer, more trusting relationship with Jude. This is your long-term goal and intention. So it doesn't serve your purpose to create unnecessary stress—the emphasis being on unnecessary. Sports stuff scattered around is not a deal breaker; it's just bothersome.

There are, after all, many issues in life that are inevitably stressful. It's not wise to create frivolous ones. Accusing Jude of not keeping a promise forces him to defend himself from accusations that he's irresponsible and a liar.

Dealing with the issue effectively means finding a way to solve the problem that doesn't erode the feelings of love and tenderness that bind you together.

RULE TWO ▸ Say only what you need to say—nothing more.

Starting out with an emphatic swear word, *dammit*, is dangerous. You're using a bugle to announce your assault: Let the nastiness begin! You can expect serious blowback.

Reminding Jude that he made a promise and is now not keeping it is saying too much. It raises issues of his honesty. The immediate issue is cleaning up his stuff so you have room for your own.

RULE THREE ▸ Don't ask questions that don't have an actual answer, doesn't directly apply here.

RULE FOUR SURELY DOES ▶ Do not use blame—no criticism, accusation, punishment or humiliation.

You're definitely criticizing Jude for being irresponsible . . . at the very least.

How might he respond? Defensively, perhaps angrily. Or he'll turn inward and pout, accusing you of being a control freak or worse. He might bury his resentment until he has a chance to get even. When a person is criticized, accused, punished or humiliated, there's always some kind of negative reaction or retaliation. There's no such thing as a risk-free attack.

RULE FIVE ▶ Always be ready to stop when things get too heated.

If you have already launched a broadside of criticism and accusation, you can stop the downward spiral with an apology: *"I'm sorry, Jude. I shouldn't have attacked you that way."*

Of course it's better not to start this negative interaction at all.

So what should you say when you see a mess that shows no signs of getting organized?

SAY THIS: *"Jude, I'm upset that I don't have a place to put my things."*

That's all.

Just that? you might ask. Yes. Because this is where the first rule comes back in (as it always will), by which you ask yourself, What do I want to accomplish with this interaction? Your goal is not just getting Jude to clean up a mess; it's also to help him understand that he needs to be disciplined about his stuff because you're now both sharing the same space.

And, most important, you want to use this communication as a way to draw closer to Jude, not push him away.

Effective communication is about more than just using words to fulfill your needs, or to get something from another person. Indeed, speaking well and choosing the right words at the right time is perhaps the greatest accomplishment to which we can aspire. Consider the world's greatest author, William Shakespeare. After five hundred years, his works remain the most produced, studied and quoted. And yet—they're just words!

The ability to communicate effectively is rooted deep within your personality. If you're one of the lucky 10 percent of people who naturally connect to your inner self as you speak—and your inner self is composed of generosity, graciousness and a sense of personal responsibility—then your words and behaviors will carry you far toward success in all your endeavors.

If, however, your history (including how you were raised and what you learned in your family) has some serious gaps—if you didn't learn lots of good habits and did learn a whole bunch of bad—then teaching yourself how to communicate effectively can help reshape your personality and develop greater capacities for those three characteristics—generosity, graciousness and personal responsibility. All of which are good qualities to bring into any situation in life.

AS TIME GOES BY ... MAINTAINING WHAT YOU HAVE

Maintaining a healthy relationship presents a somewhat different set of challenges than beginning one. Let's assume that you and your partner have both decided that you're compatible enough to spend most of your nights with each other or to actually to move in together. At that point, your task switches from exploring and evaluating the relationship to maintaining it so that it continues to mature.

And that involves being an authentic adult and truly embracing the mature responsibilities of life. Every day you're together brings you closer to spending the next few decades of your life with this complicated human being. Or even until death do ye part. So the potential risks to your life-long happiness become greater.

Almost inevitably, certain negative behaviors will emerge.

NEGATIVE HABITS INCLUDE THE TENDENCIES TO:

- keep score; to measure whether you're getting what you're giving
- focus on mistakes and examine them for hidden meanings
- tighten your control over money, food, time and sex
- try to prove yourself right and reactively defend your territory

Each one of these can result in unpleasant power struggles.

And along the way, gestures of appreciation may diminish, and taking for granted set in. All these can make you feel nervous about the wisdom of your choice, and deeper questions can emerge:

"Does my partner really love and respect me?"

"Have I chosen the best possible mate?"

"Can I trust what my partner tells me?"

"Can I trust how my partner handles our finances?"

"Will my partner be there when I need emotional support?"

AND EVEN MORE COMPLEX QUESTIONS SIMMER BELOW:

"Will I continue to find him/her sexually interesting over the years?"

And, above all:

"Will we grow together as we mature or separate into parallel lives?"

And beneath those is the even deeper practical question; the one that ties them all together:

"Will we be able to work together to solve our day-to-day problems?"

A major goal of *Say This, Not That* is to help you solve ordinary day-to-day problems—the endless stream of small stuff—by finding ways to communicate effectively about them. Which in turn increases the longer-term happiness and the mutually supportive, loving qualities of your relationship.

Let's begin with the first scenes.

He's Late and Doesn't Care

THE SITUATION: *You're meeting your sweetheart, he shows up twenty minutes late and he's only vaguely apologetic.*

DON'T SAY THIS *(sarcastically):* *"Well, I'm glad you finally made it."* (Sending the wrong message: I'll make your pay for your mistake.)

BAN SARCASM: Making a sarcastic statement or asking a sarcastic question sets a verbal trap in which everyone gets caught. Sarcasm is one of the worst forms of communication because it can create confusion (Did you really mean what you said?) and makes you appear to have a harsh and critical personality. Above all, sarcasm sounds like punishment, a highly toxic form of blame.

BE CLEAR AND DIRECT. Sarcasm is neither clear nor direct. It forces the other person to try to understand your meaning and creates anxiety and resentment.

BODY LANGUAGE ALERT: Try not to convey your upset with a tight expression—narrowed eyes, furrowed brow and pursed lips. Negative facial or body language drives people crazy.

BUT DO SAY SOMETHING: Unless you truly aren't bothered by someone being late (a slippery slope that could encourage irresponsibility), don't pretend that nothing is bothering you. You need to clear the air and express your feelings—but effectively.

SAY THIS: *"It bothers me that you were late and barely mentioned it."* (Sending the right message: I deal with issues maturely.)

WHY IT WORKS: This simple statement avoids a harsh attack that creates the need for defense.

REMEMBER THIS RULE: EVERYTHING COUNTS. Every behavior means something, and you'll need to assess what each behavior means and how it will potentially influence the relationship.

WHAT DOES IT MEAN? Being late could mean the person overbooks his schedule and then rushes, or indicate a general lack of concern for other people's needs. Small behaviors can point to a submerged problem (picture an iceberg) or turn out to be inconsequential (a piece of random flotsam). Your job is to figure out which applies to each behavior. That's why—especially in the beginning of relationships—*everything counts.*

REAL-LIFE STORY: When Kiri met Bill, she felt an immediate attraction. But he had just started a new job and during their first four dates, he was late twice and had to cancel once. The last straw was when he didn't show up for a movie, or even call. Kiri decided that Bill was not ready to dedicate himself to a relationship, and stopped seeing him.

Her Mind Seems to Wander

THE SITUATION: *At your first important formal event together, Jenny frequently glances around the room and seems distracted. She answers her cell phone and begins texting a message.*

DON'T SAY *(angrily):* *"Do you think you could shut off your phone for at least a few minutes?"* (Sending the wrong message: I'm controlling and easily upset.)

HOW MIGHT THE PERSON RESPOND? This sounds like a parent scolding a teenager, and is likely to provoke an adolescent response—a sullen look, the silent treatment, excuses and justifications or just plain fury. None will help the relationship.

HARSHNESS RARELY HELPS: Direct and harsh confrontation is rarely a good idea unless you don't mind offending the other person. Anger is our most powerful emotion and even a small amount of it can be destructive.

PLAN AHEAD: Think strategically. Figure out what few words will communicate your irritation without being excessively critical, offensive or angry. When your date is obviously distracted and texts someone in your presence, that's rude. A strategic response would get your point across and express your need without unnecessarily creating a conflict that might take on a life of its own.

SAY THIS: *"Sweetie, it really bothers me when you use your cell phone a lot when we're spending time together."* Keep your facial expression positive—don't grimace or frown! (Sending the right message: I can ask for what I want without being critical.)

HOW MIGHT THE PERSON RESPOND? While no one likes to be confronted directly, making a direct request in a caring voice can be refreshing. It tells the other person, right from the beginning, that you're not a doormat. Hopefully, you'll get a positive reply: *"I'm really sorry about that."* But be ready for a reaction. If it's negative, take some time to decide on your best reply.

HONESTY ADVANCES RELATIONSHIPS: Being authentic is an essential part of an early relationship. Unless you don't actually care about it, tolerating rude or distracted behavior that annoys you does not convey an accurate idea of who you are.

DON'T OVERPERSONALIZE: Another important rule in developing a relationship: Don't take everything personally! While you may hope for blissful experiences, it's far more realistic to expect them to be less than perfect. You—and the other person—have a right to be a little awkward and do or say something less than graceful. Not taking every action personally allows you to rise above the awkwardness or even the offense.

She Came On to My Friend!

THE SITUATION: *You've just met for dinner with another couple and your girlfriend, Jessica, greets your friend Mark with a big hug and kiss on the mouth.*

DON'T SAY THIS (*with an angry frown*): *"What's that about? You guys have something going on I don't know about?"* (Sending the wrong message: You're a cheat and I'm ready to tell the world.)

MISTAKE: Calling attention to an embarrassing behavior creates a drama that might quickly get out of control. You *must* discuss this in private.

HOW MIGHT THE PERSON RESPOND? Defensively! "What's your problem?" Or aggressively: "You sure are uptight!" Or passively, lapsing into an angry silence.

DON'T MAKE THINGS WORSE: Just as in medicine—where the first rule is to do no harm—the first concern in communication is *Don't make things worse.* Before causing a scene or creating a memorable mess, remember the First Rule of Effective Communication and ask yourself: What do you want to accomplish? If the answer doesn't come to you immediately, pause, say nothing for a moment and think about it.

SUSPEND JUDGMENT: Being highly affectionate in public is not automatically a sign of promiscuity. It could be about loose boundaries. If you really think that she's really trying to set something up with Mark and that the kiss is sexual behavior, you've got a big problem. Have a *private* heart-to-heart talk.

SAY THIS: *"I'm so glad to see you"* (to everyone). Ignore the kiss! (Sending the right message: I'm not easily provoked.)

SIMPLY DECIDE: You're an adult: A simple kiss, a little excessive affection is not going to faze you. You're making a strategic decision to not overreact.

BUT AGAIN, EVERYTHING COUNTS: Remember the concept discussed in the dating section: EVERYTHING COUNTS? If this incident is overt enough to raise an actual red flag, pay attention. It's easy to get so caught up in the excitement of being social that we forget to pay attention to what our partner is doing. You need to know whether your girlfriend gives all her male friends a kiss on the mouth—and if she does, what it means.

HOW TO APPROACH IT: If you are sincerely bothered by Jessica's behavior, choose a good time to tell Jessica calmly that so much overt affection troubles you. Listen to her explanation. Most relatively simple situations can be resolved with a heart-to-heart talk. Furthermore, resolving relatively momentary issues sets you up for success in solving more complex problems when they appear.

I'm Being Totally Ignored

THE SITUATION: *You attend a party with your boyfriend and he doesn't introduce you to other people. You're angry and hurt.*

DON'T SAY THIS: *"If you're going to ignore me, I'm leaving!"* while glaring and then dramatically heading for the door. (Sending the wrong message: I'm super-sensitive and impulsive.)

MISTAKE: You are overreacting. Now the focus will be on your sudden outraged departure rather than on your boyfriend's discourtesy.

ANGER ESCALATES: Whenever you react angrily to an offense, the anger charges your body with adrenaline. Your facial expression changes visibly, as do your posture and other body language. Your partner cannot help but see and feel these changes, and his body will automatically be flooded with adrenaline to protect him from your anger. Which means that he'll also get angry. Now both of you are angry. Not helpful.

BEWARE OF FLARING: Anger is our most dangerous emotion and must be indulged in sparingly. Far too often we get angry over imaginary slights. In this case, perhaps your boyfriend gets nervous and distracted at parties and simply doesn't remember to introduce you. While that doesn't justify his behavior, it's a factor to consider as you decide how to handle the situation.

SAY THIS: Reach out your hand and introduce yourself with a smile. *"Hi, my name is . . ."* (Sending the right message: I know how to handle a social blunder.)

ALWAYS BE STRATEGIC: Before reacting to any offense, take time to consider the consequences of your behavior. The most successful people in relationships and in life are those who think and act strategically. Synonyms of *strategic* are *planned, considered, deliberate.* All these require thinking about how your behavior—what you deliberately plan to do—will help you fulfill your needs. Then choose a behavior that advances your goals.

REAL-LIFE STORY: When Ravi invited Sharmilla to a party at his company headquarters, she knew he was a successful engineer but little else about him. When he became involved in a conversation with a colleague and ignored her, Sharmilla waited until after the party and gently confronted him about his behavior. "I know you're good at your job," she said, "but if you want to be with me, I need to be . . ."—she smiled warmly—"*almost* as important as your work. If I'm not, I'd rather spend time with other friends." Ravi got the message and, with Sharmilla's firm but gentle coaching, learned how to include her.

I'll Punish Her with Silence

THE SITUATION: *Angie is too busy to get together because her cousin's coming to visit.*

DON'T DO THIS: *Give her the silent treatment. Don't return her calls. Show her that you're more important than some cousin!* (Sending the wrong message: I can't be trusted to work together to resolve issues.)

IT'S PASSIVE-AGGRESSIVE: While it's reasonable to be upset because it seems that Angie put someone else before you, withdrawing into angry silence is being "passive-aggressive"—controlling others through deliberate inaction.

IT'S A DEAD END: It's destructive in three ways: (1) You're punishing her by sulking and refusing to engage, and punishment invites retribution. (2) The issue simmers and tension builds, which generates resentment. (3) You're creating a power struggle over which one of you will break down first.

AVOID POWER STRUGGLES: Power struggles tend to take on a life of their own, creating an ever more dramatic contest for dominance. They're dangerous to any relationship. "I don't care what you want; I won't address this issue until I'm good and ready" is just a way of saying, "You disappoint me and I'll make you pay!" This behavior creates resentment and eventual retaliation, because no long-lasting relationship can tolerate continued high levels of resentment.

SAY THIS: *"I'm really upset about not being able to get together. Let's talk about it as soon as possible."* (Sending the right message: I'm willing to solve this problem.)

CONFLICT TAKES COURAGE: Rarely does a relationship move along without some form of conflict. In fact, if there's no conflict, one of the parties must be yielding on every issue. And that spells the death of the relationship. So telling your partner that you're upset and then asking to talk about it requires a high level of emotional courage.

DIRECT IS BEST: Research on conflict shows that addressing an issue directly produces the best results. In almost all cases the conflict is because of different perceptions, erroneous assumptions and confusion about communications. Only when you sit down and calmly discuss the problem can you reach a mutual understanding.

TALKING ABOUT FAMILY: Every healthy relationship must come to an agreement about how to handle family obligations. And the only way to reach an agreement is to discuss it—sometimes over and over. The perfect solution usually takes time and multiple discussions to work out.

Don't Tell Me What to Do!

THE SITUATION: *You're upset by a friend's behavior and your boyfriend tells you that your way of handling it is all wrong.*

DON'T SAY THIS: *"Who are you to talk? You let your friends walk all over you!"* (Sending the wrong message: I will punish anyone who makes me feel bad.)

MISTAKE: Even though his advice implies that you're less than competent, blurting out an accusation will only lead to retaliation.

FRIENDS IMPACT COUPLES: When you're in a committed relationship, each of you *will* have to give and receive advice. Because the behavior of your friends affects you both, you need to be able to give each other constructive feedback about it. Otherwise, friends might exert excessive negative influence, contaminating your relationship.

DISCUSSING FRIENDS IS INEVITABLE: How you and your partner manage your other relationships can contribute to or detract from your happiness. Each of you will have to determine how influential your friends will be in your relationships, and how much time each of you spends in their company. It's all but inevitable that there will be some level of conflict, especially if a friend has a negative impact.

SAY THIS: *"I know you get upset when my friend acts like this, but I want to deal with it in my own way."* (Sending the right message: I appreciate your concern but I want to handle the situation.)

BOUNDARIES ARE CRUCIAL: Telling another person directly that you want to deal with a problem yourself is one form of setting a firm boundary. Preventing unwanted incursions into your life will help you achieve enduring happiness. This includes other people's criticisms, accusations and negative behaviors.

ADVICE CAN BE TRICKY: Giving and receiving advice are some of our most complicated interactions. Being able to give advice in a way that respects another person's sense of competence is an advanced skill. So is being able to listen to your partner's suggestions with an open mind.

RELATIONSHIPS ARE NOT SOLO ACTS: There's no such thing in a committed relationship as constructively saying, "Leave me alone, I want to do everything myself." If that's your attitude, then stay single.

DON'T HAVE STRONG BOUNDARIES? Healthy boundaries can be developed. If you grew up in a family that didn't teach you about how to protect yourself emotionally as well as physically, you can learn those skills. That begins with understanding how boundaries work. For more information about boundaries, consult the "Advanced Work" section at the end of the book.

I Get Wounded Easily

THE SITUATION: *You're with your sweetheart and friends, and your sweetheart makes a critical comment about your job. You take it person-ally and feel intense shame. Your evening is ruined.*

DON'T SAY THIS *(to yourself)*: *"What's wrong with me?"* and then get angry and pout. (Sending yourself the wrong message: I'm too fragile to deal with life.)

LETTING IN TOO MUCH: You actually have a choice about what you're going to let inside and what you're going to keep out. To think otherwise is to allow yourself to be a victim of what could simply be good-natured teasing.

SHOWING WOUNDS TO OTHERS: Reacting publicly and dramatically to a per-ceived offense is risky. You can send the message to others that you're easily wounded, and they are likely to feel on edge around you, afraid of saying some-thing you might take the wrong way. If you overreact with your sweetheart in this situation, he or she might not trust your emotional stability. A relationship cannot thrive if either person feels constantly responsible for taking care of the other's highly sensitive feelings.

DON'T CONFRONT PUBLICLY: The wisest and most strategic decision is to wait until you're alone (or even the next day) to bring up something that happened in front of other people. Of course, we're talking about a teasing comment, not a flagrant insult, which we'll deal with in a following scene.

SAY THIS *(to yourself)*: *"I'm mature enough to deal with this later."* Then smile. (Sending the right message: I'm not a fragile child.)

STRENGTHEN YOUR BOUNDARIES: The ongoing theme of all these scripts is to think about the best thing to say at the best time. Developing your "emotional boundaries" is part of this work.

HOW EMOTIONAL BOUNDARIES HELP: People say and do things every day that can be hurtful. Emotional boundaries act like an invisible force field to protect you from feelings, ideas and behaviors that don't really apply to you, or that you can't do anything about.

ASK YOURSELF: *"What can I do about this right now?"* Since 95 percent of the time, right in that moment, there's nothing you can do, saying this to yourself will strengthen your emotional boundaries and protect you from irresponsible comments and behaviors beyond your control.

LONG-TERM TIP: Having strong emotional boundaries is essential to developing fulfilling long-term relationships. Unfortunately, there's no magic potion to strengthen them. It takes focused attention and a determination to not overreact. Over time you'll feel stronger and tougher. For more on this, see the "Boundaries" segment in the "Advanced Work" section at the end of this book.

Why Are You So Grouchy?

THE SITUATION: *Your girlfriend comes home in a sullen, grouchy mood. Within seconds you're feeling upset at her for ruining your evening.*

DON'T SAY THIS *(accusingly)*: *"Geez, what's wrong with you?"* (Sending the wrong message: I can't deal with any uncomfortable feelings.)

DON'T CRITICIZE PEOPLE'S FEELINGS: The above question is both a criticism and an accusation. Criticism and accusation always feel like personal attacks and provoke a Reactive Response, which in turn will set off an argument.

REMEMBER YOUR RESPONSIBILITY: Your job is to be supportive of your partner's feelings, even if the emotion may seem exaggerated, silly, useless, etc. To imply otherwise will make your partner feel as though she can't trust you to deal with uncomfortable situations.

DON'T LET OTHERS' FEELINGS OVERWHELM YOU: When we care about another person, we also care about their feelings . . . and their struggles. But jumping into their emotional swimming pool is never a good idea: Now you're both wet! If you have healthy emotional boundaries, you won't allow yourself to be taken over by another's feelings. You need to maintain your own emotional independence so that you can express empathy, but not resentment. Without empathy, there can be no authentic closeness.

SAY THIS: *"I'm sorry you're feeling down. Is there something you'd like to talk about?"* (Sending the right message: I'm strong enough to handle your feelings.)

PRACTICE CLOSENESS, NOT DISTANCE: There's no such thing as a correct or incorrect feeling (except for rage—excessive anger expressed through screaming or violence—for which there's no justification). When caught up in any emotion, we all need someone to hear us and acknowledge our feelings. We especially want the people closest to us to understand what we're going through, or least make an effort. The more sincere the effort, the more people will feel loved.

LOVE IS A VERB: To love means to put forth a sincere effort to understand the other person's reality. You don't have to act like a therapist and say something to "cure" the situation. All you need to do is be present and available to listen.

THE MIRACLE OF LISTENING: Countless stories attest to the healing power of a good listener. It doesn't take skill; it simply requires a willingness to be present. This willingness is instantly understood as love. If listening attentively doesn't come easily to you, however, keep in mind that it is a skill that you can learn how to be a better listener . . . and it gets easier with the first sign of success.

He Spent All Our Savings!

THE SITUATION: *Your boyfriend comes home with a big new TV even as both of you struggle to meet household bills. "But we deserve it!" he protests.*

DON'T SAY THIS: *"You're such a baby—you have no self-control!"* (Sending the wrong message: He's a spoiled brat and you're stupid for staying with him.)

BE ON THE ALERT FOR SPENDING PROBLEMS: This behavior might be a deal breaker, because you don't want to continue in a relationship with someone who has no financial self-discipline. You *must* solve this problem.

COULD BE AN ADDICTION: Spending money on nonessentials threatens the long-term viability of any relationship, and a pattern of overspending can signal a shopping addiction, which can be as destructive as any other. Active addictions threaten the trust that's the lifeblood of committed relationships. If you're looking toward eventual marriage, you must deal with this in a serious, methodical way that produces a solution.

CONTROLLING IMPULSES: We're constantly barraged by images of things we "need" to buy. While maintaining a budget is not easy, it's crucial to any partnership's long-term success. Impulse control is the key.

SAY THIS: *"That's a big purchase. I'm worried about our budget. We need to sit down and talk about this."* (Sending the right message: I recognize the problem and intend to solve it.)

PRACTICE PATIENCE: It can often take numerous discussions to come to agreements on spending—but it's worth the time.

FACE FINANCIAL PROBLEMS FIRST: Problems involving money—whether overspending or underspending (compulsive frugality) so profoundly affect partnerships that I've often advised my patients to *solve financial problems first.*

COMMIT TO CONTROL SPENDING: Solving money problems might involve making a monthly budget—and scheduling monthly reviews of how well you're sticking to it. Out-of-control situations might require a financial adviser. Some couples struggle so fiercely over spending that they'll need formal counseling. Regardless, don't ignore ongoing money issues—they affect everything else in life.

AGREEING TO DISAGREE: Couples don't have to agree on everything, but if they don't, they must be respectful about disagreements. Successful couples have numerous techniques for resolving problems, and *must* have effective methods in place to help them maintain and strengthen their emotional, sexual, financial and social connections to each other over time.

CONSTRUCTIVE CONFLICT: One highly effective process is called Constructive Conflict. The following scene describes a part of this process. (Refer to the "Constructive Conflict" segment in the "Advanced Work" section at the end of this book for greater detail.)

And It's Your Fault!

THE SITUATION: *You're rushing off to work; there's no milk for your cereal.*

DON'T SAY THIS: *"Dammit, Myra, can't you even keep milk in the house?"* (Sending the wrong message: She's so incompetent she can't even buy groceries.)

MISTAKE: Too strong a reaction. Running out of a food item does not mean you have the right to act like a grumpy adolescent or launch into blame.

CONSIDER IT A TEST: Countless relationship events will test your character and personality. If you let minor inconveniences set off inflexible responses, the chance of the relationship's achieving long-term success is greatly in doubt.

BAN BLAME: Saying the above is a classic example of blame, which includes four destructive behaviors: criticism, accusation, punishment and humiliation. Any and all of these negative and toxic behaviors erode trust and create resentment. If continued, they will lead to animosity and eventually to separation. While it takes rigorous effort to not use blame, there are ways to express your needs and feelings without using it, which you'll find richly rewarded with your partner's increasing trust.

SAY THIS: *"Darn, there's no milk* (sigh). *I'll pick some up on my way home."* (Sending the right message: I'm a resourceful adult.)

STICK WITH THE POSITIVE: It's sometimes tough being entirely responsible for your own emotions and reactions. But by embedding your response in a positive context, namely "I'm resourceful, and we're both responsible for groceries," a missing food item becomes a simple problem to solve rather than an occasion for indulging in blame—which always drives people further apart.

FOCUS ON YOUR BASIC NEED: Knowing what you truly need at the moment will help you make the best decisions when responding to daily events. In this case, an angry scene about missing milk is *not* what you need right before going off to work. Nor will it do anything to create a collaborative environment for assuring future grocery supplies.

AND WHAT YOU NEED NOW IS: Serenity and focus for the workday ahead. So express your frustration in a calm, respectful way, and then get on with your day.

HOW TO KNOW IF IT'S A BASIC NEED: Just about anything that advances your "long-term best interests" is a basic need. So eating a brownie before bed does not fit into that category. Nor does getting into a useless and harmful argument. Keeping your relationship warm and cordial, on the other hand, does.

You're Canceling Our Date?

THE SITUATION: *Your boyfriend cancels your anniversary date because of work.*

DON'T SAY THIS: *"I can't believe that your work's more important than me!"* (Sending the wrong message: I'll force you to choose between your career and me.)

PICKING THE WRONG FIGHT: While it's logical that you're feeling disappointed and even angry, you need to find out the facts before you react. If you and your boyfriend have an open and honest relationship, then you need to trust that he was forced to cancel your date for a good reason. If he doesn't have one, finding out what's going on is more important than fuming.

NOT ALL CHOICES ARE EASY: Life is not really just one thing (work/career) or the other (love/devotion). A healthy life requires creating a balance between commitments. Couples often get into trouble when one person tries to emphasize one area (work, saving money, sex, socializing, recreation) at the expense of another. This includes demanding that your partner show love or commitment in a very specific way.

LOOK FOR THE GOOD: Your boyfriend may have many ways of showing he loves you. Each partner in a relationship needs to practice flexibility about how the other handles other commitments and demonstrates devotion.

SAY THIS: *"I'm really disappointed. Let's talk later."* (Sending the right message: I'm adult enough to handle disappointments.)

A WISE RESPONSE: This statement is mature and smart. It's mature because it allows you to express your feelings while not punishing your partner. It's smart because you're inviting a discussion about the event at a later time.

FULFILLING YOUR BASIC NEED: Your basic need in this situation (and in your overall relationship) is to develop long-term fulfillment. Developing a fulfilling relationship doesn't typically happen without serious effort, which explains why some 50 percent of marriages fail. The most difficult challenge in all relationships is to *not* respond with blame when your desires are frustrated. Blame, which is really criticism and accusation, only makes things worse. It does not advance your long-term interests.

AN OPPORTUNITY FOR BETTER PLANNING: Use this disappointment as an opportunity to discuss your mutual needs and find ways to avoid future problems. Perhaps your boyfriend could plan his work schedule more carefully. Maybe you need to recognize that there will be ongoing last-minute scheduling conflicts with his job. At the very least, he can alert you to the possibility of canceling a date because of pressure at work. Better advance planning can make all the difference in the outcome.

But You Said You Wanted Sex

THE SITUATION: *Just when you expected to have sex your partner says she's too tired.*

DON'T SAY THIS (*angrily*): *"You only think about yourself!"* (Sending the wrong message: I will punish you if I'm disappointed.)

MISTAKE: Your frustration makes you want to strike back. You've somehow come to believe that your partner should be available for sex even when she's tired and therefore unwilling. Now your strong reaction will create yet more problems.

INTIMIDATION RUINS INTIMACY: The above reaction will likely intimidate your partner. Now she'll probably worry about how you'll react in the future if she doesn't feel emotionally or physically available for making love.

GOOD SEX IS A BASIC NEED: Sex and all forms of physical intimacy are a basic need for happiness. Furthermore, sexual intimacy forms a large part of how couples build long-term, fulfilling relationships. But a loving, satisfying sex life is not guaranteed just because you're sexually attracted to each other.

HANDLE SEXUAL ISSUES GENTLY: There are so many variables and so many ways for either party to upset the other that couples need to be very careful—*repeat: very careful*—about dealing with sex. Your basic need in this case is evident: to create a loving environment in which both of your sexual needs can be fulfilled.

SAY THIS: *"Darn, I was really in the mood to be close to you. I'm disappointed."* That's all! (Sending the right message: I can communicate frustration without punishing you.)

EXPRESS, DON'T CONDEMN: This statement declares the obvious, but without criticizing. It's far less likely to trigger a Reactive Response. Which means that there's a far better chance of discussing the issue and coming to a caring and rewarding resolution.

A BASIC RULE: Always do everything you can to avoid creating a negative reaction. Anger and fear raise blood pressure, increase heart rate and increase the chance of an ongoing conflict.

TAKES TWO TO TURN ON: When your partner declines to have sex for whatever reason, you need to consider the most important issue—which is *always* maintaining a loving and trusting connection. For sex to help create love and trust, it must be a consensual expression of affection. Which means that the conditions must be right for both partners.

BUILDING TRUST: Ask yourself, "What are my long-term best interests in this situation?" The answer: to deepen the relationship by building trust. Because great sexual experiences accomplish so much for both partners, handling every potential sexual encounter with exquisite care is highly recommended.

I Just Can't Trust You, Can I?

THE SITUATION: *Laurie had agreed to call the landlord about problems with the plumbing. A week later nothing's happened. She insists that you said that you'd call.*

DON'T SAY: *"I obviously can't trust you to follow through on your word."* (Sending the wrong message: She's a flake.)

MISTAKE: Way too harsh and accusatory. Every word of this outburst is wrong. Unless you want to end up alone, don't verbally attack your partner in accusatory tones.

A TRIPLE THREAT: This is a flagrant use of blame. It employs both criticism and accusation. You're criticizing Laurie for not making a simple phone call, implying overall incompetence. You're accusing her of being untrustworthy, a very serious charge. You're asserting, by using the term *obviously*, that this issue is constant and that you've given up. If you really believe all this, why are you with her?

BAN BLAME: Blame has no part in any relationship because it instantly triggers an RR, a Reactive Response. It feels so bad to be blamed—to be criticized and accused—that the only responses will be anger and retaliation. Using blame in your communications will sabotage every past attempt you've made to build the relationship. It's crucial to learn how to communicate without resorting to criticism, accusation, punishment or humiliation.

SAY THIS: *"Let's not get into who was supposed to call the landlord. Can you do it today?"* (Sending the right message: I want to focus on the solution, not on blame.)

MEMORIES CAN MISLEAD: A basic rule in relationships—never argue about perception and memory. Because it's extremely unlikely that you have a videotape of the original conversation, it's fruitless to insist that your memory is correct. Studies show that many things influence memory. Even when people do see or hear recordings of who actually said what, they still often disagree about what actually happened. So don't argue about it.

FOCUS ON FIXING IT: Domestic tranquility requires not getting stuck in futile discussions. Focus your energy not on proving the other person wrong, but on solving the problem. Couples who follow a more constructive approach will live a longer and happier life.

REAL-LIFE STORY: Johanna and Javier come from different cultural and linguistic backgrounds (namely, German and Spanish), so they tend to see things based on their own cultural backgrounds as well as from their own personal perspectives. After a spate of increasingly volatile arguments, they designed a series of "code words" to describe each other's worldview. Now when one of them makes a mistake or forgets something, the other can lightly refer to it as "the German (or Spanish) version of reality." This jocular approach avoids criticism, spares either of them from accusation and rapidly defuses tension. Most misunderstandings end in smiles.

How About Some Appreciation?

THE SITUATION: *You get home from work, spend an hour cleaning up the kitchen and suddenly your partner pops in and asks: "You making anything for dinner?"*

DON'T SAY THIS (angrily): *"So cleaning up this pigsty of a kitchen isn't enough for you?"* (Sending the wrong message: I need appreciation and I'll punish you if I don't get it.)

MISTAKE: While it's natural to want to feel appreciated, this approach won't help.

HOW CAN THE PERSON RESPOND? You're virtually guaranteeing a Reactive Response: *"I didn't ask you to clean the kitchen!"* or *"If you're going to be such a jerk about it, then don't even bother cleaning!"*

ACCUSATIONS ALWAYS AGGRAVATE: Using criticism to address your feelings of being unappreciated always carries you further away from solving a problem. It also guarantees that you won't hear kind words in return.

A GUARANTEED BAD OUTCOME: Snapping back, especially in an accusatory manner, doesn't encourage appreciation. It also doesn't resolve any ongoing problems involving equitable sharing of chores. Deciding how to share household duties—who is responsible for what tasks and when—requires a more mature approach.

SAY THIS (*calmly*): *"Honey, before you ask me about dinner, please notice what I've been doing."* (Sending the right message: I know what I need and I'm capable of asking for it directly.)

AND YET IT STILL MIGHT GET COMPLICATED: Although this is a direct, positive statement about your needs, your partner may still hear it as subtle blaming: *"You're calling me insensitive."* And respond, *"I've been working my butt off all day, too!"* If said aggressively, they're issuing an invitation to do battle.

STAY ON MESSAGE: Don't engage! If you get a defensive or attacking response, just repeat your message: You wish to hear appreciation for what you do. If one of you has forgotten to express appreciation, simply admit it: You'll try to do better next time.

KEEP CALM REGARDLESS: What do you want to accomplish when you ask for appreciation? You want to communicate your need for acknowledgment. No matter what response your partner gives, stay calm and focused on your goal. *Staying calm is always the key.*

IF NEEDED, TAKE TIME OUT: Keep in mind that you can always ask for a time-out. Having an agreement in place allowing for conversations to stop when things take a turn for the worse must be part of every couple's communicational tool kit. See the "Please, Stop!" segment in the "Advanced Work" section at the end of this book.

I'm So Glad You Had a Chance to Rest

THE SITUATION: *You had agreed to do a chore but, feeling fatigued, take a nap instead. Your partner makes a sarcastic comment about your taking time for yourself.*

DON'T SAY THIS: *"Well, you're the one who sat in front of the TV all day Sunday!"* or *"Just because you're a workaholic doesn't mean I have to be."* (Sending the wrong message: I'll punish you for criticizing me.)

MISTAKE: Responding to an angry accusation with another angry attack guarantees a nasty scene. In relationships, fighting fire with more fire only builds toward a flaming conflagration. Cooling actions are what you need instead.

SKIP THE SARCASM: Sarcasm has no place in any relationship. Almost without exception sarcasm conveys criticism: There's something wrong with you . . . try to figure out what it is! In this case, your partner could be resentful that you took a nap while he couldn't allow himself to relax. He may be using sarcasm because he doesn't know how to take care of his own needs (and resents that you do), and/or doesn't know how to communicate his feelings respectfully.

SARCASM NEVER SERVES: Sarcasm is a low form of humor and very rarely funny. At the very least it's irritating. Even the common retort "Duh!" to an obvious fact can sound critical and accusatory if used too often or at the wrong moment.

SAY THIS: *"Sometimes I need to nap. You can do the same when you need one."* (Sending the right message: I can turn your criticism into a constructive statement.)

SMART AND SUPPORTIVE: This response gets right to the point. You're saying exactly what needs to be said, both about your own needs, and those of your partner.

HOW MIGHT HE RESPOND? This comment is so direct and to the point that he will likely be taken aback by its sincerity. Most important, you're not taking the bait, not responding in kind, and are, in fact, completely avoiding his resentment-soaked taunt and expressing your generous wish for him to take care of himself.

GENEROSITY ALWAYS WINS: Reacting generously to a criticism is the best way to score two goals with one ball. First, you're avoiding a fight by not responding in kind. Second, you're "teaching" the other person a "higher" way of expressing a feeling or a need.

IT'S TOUGH, BUT WORTH IT: Acting with generosity requires a solid emotional foundation. It's not easy to do when you feel attacked. But the biblical passage about "turning the other cheek" specifically suggests reacting to a criticism or insult with kindness. A generous response to an accusation is universally admired.

Okay! I Get It Already!

THE SITUATION: *As your girlfriend orders cheesecake for dessert, you say something about her diet. She's angry and asks you to apologize. You make a weak apology but she won't let go of the issue and repeats herself until finally you explode.*

DON'T SAY THIS (loudly): *"Why are you such a nag? I already said I was sorry! Do you want me to put it in writing?"* (Sending the wrong message: It doesn't take much for both of us to get out of control.)

ACCUSATIONS AUTO-ESCALATE: Once the process of mutual accusation begins, each person's RRs, Reactive Responses, will escalate. As each of your bodies begins to flood with adrenaline, preparing you for fight or flight, your ability to think clearly is inevitably compromised.

AVOID DAMAGING MEMORIES: Emotionally bruising arguments in which partners repeatedly yell at each other can be deeply damaging to their relationship. When the argument takes on a life of its own, it's difficult to stop the negative momentum. Later, when the damage has been done, the couple can hardly remember what the fight was about. But they do remember their emotional bruises. When a rancorous argument breaks out, the wise couple learns how to stop hitting the Blame Ball over the net.

SAY THIS: *"I'm sorry for hurting your feelings. You don't have to repeat yourself."* (Sending the right message: I don't have to lose my temper to tell you to back off.)

IF NEEDED: If, and only if, this isn't enough, add—in as quiet a volume and as neutral a tone as possible—"Please, stop."

AGREEING TO STOP: Wise couples set limits to their angry exchanges. Whenever you get caught up in a feedback loop, you must limit how many times you'll repeat the same (or similar) accusations. Each party in a relationship needs to agree to certain rules about expressing ideas and sharing feelings; that is, giving feedback.

AND THAT MEANS YOU, TOO: When you feel yourself beginning to boil, stop what you're doing. And stop completely.

THE "PLEASE, STOP" RULE: Every relationship needs an agreement that requires both partners to immediately stop talking when either hears those words. When either party gets so close to the point of overwhelm that angry accusations fly and rage zombies are set loose, either person must be able to call a halt. Later, when both have calmed down, you can discuss the issue. See the "Please, Stop!" and "Constructive Conflict" segments in the "Advanced Work" section at the end of this book for help in safely discussing volatile issues.

I'm Positive It Was on Wednesday

THE SITUATION: *Your boyfriend insists that you hadn't told him about changing an appointment to Wednesday—and can't make it.*

DON'T SAY THIS: *"Can't you remember something as simple as the days of the week?"* (Sending the wrong message: He's irresponsible and untrustworthy.)

HOW CAN HE RESPOND? After that kind of critical attack, don't be surprised if he responds with either cold, silent resentment or escalates the dispute with his own assault. It won't feel good for either of you. That kind of argument does not bring you closer, let alone solve the problem.

DON'T SWEAT SIMPLE ERRORS: A common mistake couples make is arguing over who's right or wrong about remembering a fact. Not everything you hear is automatically locked into an easily retrievable memory bank. So it's best to avoid this kind of fruitless dispute. Part of relating to others is tolerating their mistakes and misunderstandings.

CONSIDER HOW OFTEN IT OCCURS: If your partner frequently forgets important events, you both need to resolve the issue for the relationship to prosper. Frequent forgetfulness and disorganization may be signs of deeper problems that need attention.

SAY THIS: *"I'm fairly sure I told you about changing the appointment. We need to find a way to communicate more clearly."* (Sending the right message: We can work together.)

NO BLAME INVOLVED: These sentences state the problem without criticizing or accusing. They de-escalate the tension, allowing an opportunity to solve the problem peacefully.

A GOOD GENERAL RULE: Every successful relationship has rules about how partners will interact with each other. One of the most helpful rules is to not get into an argument over memory or perception. These are things subject to interpretation and distortion. The wise couple avoids arguments over who said what to whom and when. Memory is just too fluid and subject to interpretation.

EXPRESSING ANGER WITHOUT DOING DAMAGE: A critical question in all relationships is how can each person express feelings, especially anger, in a way that's both satisfying and doesn't cause harm. Anger (frustrations, irritation, etc.) is such a volatile and harmful emotion that it must always be treated as though it's radioactive. That is, with extreme care.

Why Does It Always Have to Be Your Way?

THE SITUATION: *Jeff wants to go camping on their vacation but his wife prefers to stay at her family's vacation house. They're locked in a power struggle.*

DON'T SAY THIS: Jeff: *"Fine! If you want to stay with your family, you'll have to go alone!"* (Sending the wrong message: If I can't have it my way, I won't go at all.)

ESCALATION MAKES THINGS WORSE: This statement is a threat that will either provoke more threats or result in resentful compliance. The inevitable result? An escalation into more intense accusations—or a sharp decrease in closeness. No one likes to be threatened or dominated or given unpleasant options.

AVOIDING A REACTIVE RESPONSE: The idea of not saying or doing something that triggers a physical response is woven into many situations in this book. That's because we *must* respond with our physical bodies. Our blood pressure and heart rate rule our lives! Thinking clearly becomes impossible when we're highly agitated.

EVERY COUPLE NEEDS A WAY TO DEAL WITH CONFLICT: Research into happy relationships shows that successful couples use systems for dealing with conflict. Either they develop their own, or they use an established and proven method. A brief version of "Constructive Conflict" is described on the following page. Refer to "Advanced Work" at the end of this book for a detailed description.

SAY THIS: Jeff says: *"I want to discuss this problem in a more structured way."* (Sending the right message: I won't allow a power struggle to hurt our relationship.)

A FORMAL WAY TO ADDRESS ISSUES: Jeff's statement above may sound stiff and unnatural, but using a formal method for discussing contentious, volatile issues helps them *not* escalate into fights. It involves the following steps:

MAKE AN APPOINTMENT, TAKE TURNS: First, Jeff sets up an appointment that works for both him and his wife. They allow about twenty minutes total. They sit down and Jeff takes a few minutes to present his case. His wife commits to listening quietly and respectfully with no negative body language (no sighs or grunts). When Jeff's finished speaking, his wife has the same amount of time to speak. Jeff also listens carefully. They repeat this process twice.

A POSITIVE OUTCOME: After repeating the process only once, they come up with a compromise—they'll alternate their vacation each year. One year they'll go camping, the next they'll visit Diane's family. And they'll also take mini-vacations on their own.

MORE ON THE PROCESS: See the "Constructive Conflict" segment in "Advanced Work" at the end of this book.

Stop Your Flirting . . . or Else!

THE SITUATION: *Your boyfriend, Mike, bristles menacingly and tells you to stop flirting with a guy who's just smiled at you and you politely returned the smile.*

DON'T SAY THIS: *"Mike, if you weren't so insecure, my friendliness wouldn't bother you so much."* (Sending the wrong message: He doesn't measure up.)

HOW CAN HE RESPOND? Telling a man he's insecure—even if it might be true—is humiliating. Of blame's four behaviors (criticism, accusation, punishment and humiliation), humiliation is the most destructive. Everyone is negatively affected by humiliation, but men are especially susceptible because masculine identity is tightly connected to pride. There are really no effective ways for men to deal with humiliation. Their most typical responses are anger, rage or simmering resentment. None of which helps bring couples closer.

ALWAYS AVOID HUMILIATION: Humiliating other people—severely disrespecting them—is rarely forgotten because it attacks their basic value and self-worth. If the humiliation is especially harsh or takes place in front of others, the event can burn their memory. In relationships, that kind of severe disrespect can permanently sabotage future attempts at collaboration. In fact, nations or ethnic groups subject to ongoing humiliation will even go to war to regain their wounded pride.

SAY THIS: *"Mike, we really need to talk about you accusing me of flirting with other men and come up with a solution."* (Sending the right message: We have a serious problem and I'm willing to work on it.)

BEWARE OF JEALOUSY: Possessive jealousy can destroy a relationship. If not addressed, it can grow into a morbid paranoia that strangles the autonomy of the other person. And no person denied a large degree of emotional and physical independence will be happy.

TALK OPENLY ABOUT AFFECTION TOWARD OTHERS: Negotiating jealousy issues means working to agree on what's balanced and moderate. What are your personal limits with affection shown to others? How can each person be friendly and affectionate without going over the limit and being flirtatious? How much can each of you tolerate? Which behaviors drive you crazy? Every successful couple agrees upon limits that work for both partners.

REAL-LIFE STORY: Jerry and Crystal would get into a nasty argument after every party because Jerry would become upset whenever Crystal left his side and began talking with others, especially men. Crystal insisted they get into couples' therapy to address the issue. It took several sessions for Jerry to realize that he'd developed an overly possessive attitude about everything in his life, including his work. Over the next few months, Jerry changed many of his attitudes, and Crystal became more sensitive about being too demonstrative—and both changes resulted in a far stronger relationship.

I Have a Right to Be Angry!

THE SITUATION: *You get really angry when your fiancé leaves his wet towel on the floor.*

DON'T SAY THIS: *"Do you think you're living in a pigsty? Grow up!"* (Sending the wrong message: Something's wrong with you for being sloppy.)

INSULTS NEVER WORK: Any form of name-calling or insult is guaranteed to provoke a Reactive Response. Your brain interprets a verbal attack as a form of physical attack, and your body will respond as though you're in danger. The inevitable result: a negative reaction.

THE "CONTROL-FREAK" SYNDROME: Problems like finding a wet towel on the floor *(again!)* can provoke anxiety about whether your partner truly cares about your standards, and challenge your sense of control over your own domestic world. Living together inevitably provokes these kinds of anxiety, because no person can fully satisfy another's needs at all times. But since having control over everything is a delusion, the only reasonable approach is adult-style negotiation to reach an agreement that works for both parties.

YOU CAN'T COERCE COOPERATION: Attempts to exert control through coercion—or using blame to criticize and humiliate—are both futile and counterproductive.

SAY THIS: *"Seeing wet towels on the floor makes me feel like our home is messy and disordered. Can you please pick up your towel?"* (Sending the right message: I don't overreact with anger when I'm irritated.)

HOW CAN HE RESPOND? The typical concern about such a simple and non-confrontational message is that your words are not strong enough to get your fiancé to change his behavior. In fact, since it's a respectful invitation to change a behavior and not an edict, your fiancé now has an *opportunity* to please you by cleaning up after himself.

WE OFTEN CHOOSE TO BE ANGRY: Anger is elective—a "subjective" emotion—which means that it's subject to choice. Some people make a career of getting angry and overreacting to the slightest irritation. But you can choose to indulge that anger by allowing your emotions to spin out of control—*or you can find ways to be less annoyed.*

REAL-LIFE STORY: Justine had just received a written reprimand at work after she responded angrily to a coworker. Fear of losing her job led her to consult a therapist and sign up for yoga classes. The breathing exercises she learned through yoga proved helpful and she felt more relaxed. When she did feel herself getting angry, she'd sit down and breathe slowly. She had successfully changed her reactive, habitual pattern of lurching automatically into anger.

So I Get a Little Angry . . .

THE SITUATION: *You're driving with your girlfriend when another car cuts you off. In a rage you follow the car, swearing and honking your horn. Your girlfriend is terrified.*

DON'T SAY THIS: *"That bastard cut me off!"* (Sending the wrong message: I throw a tantrum when upset—I can't be trusted to act like an adult.)

MISTAKE: Living with the belief that you have the right to get even with people who make errors is a serious mistaken belief and a dangerous way to live. It's dangerous not only for you, because serious accidents occur during all kinds of incidents involving rage, but it's terrifying for everyone around you. Frightening people you care about cannot—*repeat, cannot*—contribute to happiness.

ANGER MAY BE JUSTIFIED, BUT RAGE ISN'T: We are neurologically wired to react strongly when our lives or those of our loved ones are threatened. Rage is a survival reaction. It's extreme anger using violence, either verbal (yelling, screaming) or physical (pushing, hitting). But slipping from irritation to anger to rage because we're offended is extremely irresponsible. And 99.9 percent of the time it's just not necessary. Perhaps no other behavior undermines trust more than watching someone rage.

SAY THIS: *"I really hate it when someone drives like a jerk."* That's all. (Sending the right message: even when provoked, I can control myself.)

REVOKING YOUR PERMISSION TO RAGE: Because the only reason to rage is to protect your life, you need to stop giving yourself permission to crank up the volume from irritation all the way to rage. The first step is serious self-talk. Your thinking must control your emotions. If it doesn't, you'll get into more and more serious trouble.

SAY TO YOURSELF: Repeat this as often as necessary: *"I can express anger without upsetting people."* You can amplify the effects of the self-message by adding: *"Everyone—even me—has the right to make a mistake."*

SLOW BREATHING—A LIFESAVER: A proven technique when you're getting upset—when you can tell that your heartbeat is accelerating—is to deliberately slow down your breathing . . . *before* your pulse shoots off the charts! Count to five as you slowly inhale and exhale. Research proves that it's virtually impossible to get very angry when you focus on breathing slowly. It's a simple technique that can save your relationship . . . and maybe your life.

I Know What You're Thinking

THE SITUATION: *You ask your boyfriend to attend a dinner with your family but he avoids giving an answer.*

DON'T SAY THIS: *"It's obvious you don't care about spending time with my family."* (Sending the wrong message: You're selfish and unloving.)

MISTAKE: Assigning your boyfriend uncaring, selfish motives forces him to defend himself before you even discuss the issue. You're setting up the conversation for failure in advance. Having to defend himself against accusations—which may well be untrue—is a daunting task he might consider hopeless.

AVOID CREATING HOPELESSNESS: A feeling of hopelessness is dangerous for any relationship. Anytime you tell another person that you know their real feelings or motives before actually finding out, you're creating a "hopeless" situation for the person you're accusing.

A NEGATIVE REAL-LIFE STORY: Vernon's family invited him to take a cruise. He wanted his girlfriend, Barbara, to go with him, but she showed no interest. Irritated and disappointed, Vernon decided to sign up to go on his own. As the cruise approached, Barbara was astounded to learn that Vernon had planned to go without her. "Well," he said, "I invited you but you weren't interested." Deeply hurt, she replied, "How could you imagine I didn't want to go? I was just tired when you brought it up." Vernon had to admit that he had misinterpreted her lack of enthusiasm as a refusal.

INSTEAD, SAY THIS: *"I really want you to come with me. Think about it and we'll talk later."* (Sending the right message: I can be patient while you consider my request.)

PRACTICE PATIENCE: Patience and generosity are great assets in any relationship. In this case, that means giving your partner some time to think and not rushing in to judge his feelings or motives.

IF SHE SAYS NO: If her initial reaction isn't what you wanted to hear, take time to inquire as to why. By inquiring, you'll avoid assigning her feelings or motives she may not have. And you'll also gain valuable information about the kinds of invitations she may respond to in the future.

A POSITIVE REAL-LIFE STORY: When Kevin asked Soledad to attend his mother's birthday party, she remained silent. He felt hurt and was about to withdraw the invitation when he remembered that at his last family get-together, his half-drunk uncle had made Soledad very uncomfortable. So the next day he asked, "I wonder if you're still upset at my uncle. He was a real jerk." She agreed. "He sure was." Kevin said, "Well, if he ever acts like that again, I promise I'll stop him." By putting himself on her side and sympathizing with Soledad's possible reason for not wanting to attend, Kevin showed a generosity of spirit. A day later, they discussed the invitation again and Soledad agreed to go with him.

I'm Not Upset—Yes, You Are!

THE SITUATION: *You and Shelby have a flare-up over breakfast, and when you come home, she's sitting alone, looking glum.*

DON'T SAY THIS: *"I don't understand why you're still upset about this morning."* (Sending the wrong message: I know what's wrong with you.)

NEVER ASSUME: A cardinal rule of relationships: Do not insist that you know why your partner is behaving in a particular way.

WHAT'S WRONG WITH IT: This approach is fundamentally disrespectful because it's an attempt at emotional domination. You're not only suggesting that she's feeling an inappropriate emotion (about the earlier argument) but that her feeling is somehow wrong. You're forcing her to defend both herself and her emotions. All of these behaviors add up to controlling your partner's freedom to feel, think and behave. While it may seem clear to you that your partner is upset and (more important) why, she could also be tired, hungry, worried about work or distressed for any number of reasons. Starting any conversation this way will create resentment.

MASTER TIP: Don't play the all-knowing psychic in your relationships. While it's okay to suggest you might know something, be careful about making it sound like you know. Even when you think you're sure you know what's going on with your partner, leave plenty of room to back off if your guess is wrong.

SAY THIS: *"You seem a little glum. Feel like talking for a few minutes?"* or *"Is there anything you might want to talk about?"* (Sending the right message: I'm sensitive to your feelings and available to give support.)

ABSORB YOUR ANXIETY: When you see your partner looking dejected, it's entirely natural to feel anxiety. People don't like to see someone they love in pain. But acting on your anxiety by blurting out an accusation—even a soft one—can trigger a Reactive Response. And we already know that an RR puts you both in danger.

STAY SUPPORTIVE: Offering a supportive or at least neutral comment is the best way to keep any discussion, in any situation, moving forward. Showing interest in your partner's life and feelings, and avoiding the assumption that you already know all about them, plays an enormous role in promoting closeness and happiness.

REAL-LIFE STORY: Yolanda had just started a new job and was having a tough time. But every time she'd start to speak about it, her partner, Ken, would interrupt with an assumption. "Let me guess: Someone spoke to you rudely again and you're resentful." Only when she told him firmly that she needed him to listen, not assume that he knew what she was feeling, and not say anything until she was finished, did he finally sit quietly while she spoke. He finally got that supporting her meant simply . . . listening.

Well, If That's Your Attitude

THE SITUATION: *You ask your partner to go to a movie and he starts to complain about the last movie you went to, which he hated.*

DON'T SAY THIS: *"Well, if you have such a crappy attitude, I'll go with a friend!"* (Sending the wrong message: I'll make you pay for frustrating my desires.)

FOCUS ON YOUR GOAL: Your goal is to have a night out with your partner. Just because he's starting out with a critical attitude, it does not doom you both to an argument and a lousy time. This incident calls for emotional maturity, which is the ability to tolerate anxiety in order to fulfill your needs. In this case, to spend quality time with your sweetheart. If you allow the anxiety you feel from his criticism to take over, you'll end up punishing him for being critical. Your need will be consumed in the angry argument that follows.

IMPATIENCE and IMPULSIVITY are some of the most damaging behaviors in any relationship. These behaviors can be connected to ADD, attention-deficit disorder. But whatever the source, an inability to tolerate frustration— not getting what you want the instant you want it—creates ongoing problems. Impulsive people often launch into blame when the other person doesn't fulfill their desires.

SAY THIS: *"Suppose you come with me for this movie, then you can choose the next one."* (Sending the right message: I can negotiate a solution.)

IMPORTANT: A pleasant, neutral tone of voice is essential for success. A demanding or sarcastic tone could easily turn your statement into an argument.

ANTIDOTE TO IMPATIENCE: One of the oldest techniques for controlling any impulse is to take several long, slow breaths and count to ten. This strategy really works!

YOU MIGHT GET A "NO": You must be ready to hear no for an answer and negotiate further if necessary. Because it's not possible for two people to always want the same thing at the same time, negotiation, compromise and acceptance must always be part of your repertoire.

REAL-LIFE STORY: Devin worked long hours and preferred to come home and work on restoring his classic car. Crystal managed a theater and loved live performances. At the outset of their relationship, Devin had explained that live theater wasn't his thing, but Crystal insisted. "If we want our relationship to still be thriving ten years from now, we have to share our lives." Crystal's comment took a while to sink in. "Okay," he finally said. "I'll go with you, but I want you to come with me to some classic-car rallies." Over the next months, as they went to each other's favorite activities, they developed a closer bond, which brought them deeper intimacy.

Why Won't You Go with Me?

THE SITUATION: *You try to set up a time to do something together but your partner always finds a reason not to.*

DON'T SAY THIS: *"Never mind—I'll just do everything by myself."* (Sending the wrong message: When I'm frustrated I just give up.)

MISTAKE: This is an issue that demands problem solving, not a power struggle.

GIVING IN TO FRUSTRATION: Finding ways to spend time together as a couple can be a challenge. Some couples naturally share common interests. But more typically, each person wants to do different kinds of activities, play dissimilar sports or go to movies or concerts that don't fit the partner's tastes. If not addressed proactively, this can create a widening gap.

NOTHING REPLACES SHARED TIME: Research demonstrates that the time a couple spends together strongly affects their sense of closeness and happiness. With social media proliferating and often replacing in-person activities, doing things together has become ever more difficult. The difficulty, however, does not diminish its importance.

THE PRINCIPLE: There's just no substitute for being with your partner or loved ones, in person, face-to-face.

SAY THIS: *"Being together is a priority for me. We must find a way to do it—otherwise we'll grow apart."* (Sending the right message: I know what's important for me, and for us, and I'm willing to push for it.)

ADDRESS CONFLICTS PROMPTLY: When this kind of conflict erupts in a relationship, it takes a lot of emotional maturity not to allow the differences to discourage everyone.

GIVE-AND-TAKE DATING: A proven technique for sharing time is called give-and-take dating. One person chooses an activity he or she really enjoys (their ideal thing to do that's not overly taxing or extreme) and just tells the partner when to be ready and how to dress: hiking boots, casual, jacket and tie, dressy clothes, etc. The activity itself is a surprise. The person who is "taken out" agrees to go along and be a "good sport."

ALTERNATE WHO'S LEADING: For the next date, the couple reverses the process.

DON'T GET STUCK IN A RUT: If a specific type of activity (a heavy metal concert, a six-hour ice-skating exhibition) proves too much for either partner, mix it up a bit and keep events briefer and lighter.

THE BENEFITS ARE MANY: Give-and-take dating brings new and different activities into the couple's lives, broadens each person's experiences and builds the practice of generosity and cooperation.

I'll Tell You What's Wrong

THE SITUATION: *Your partner comes home from a business meeting angry with his boss and coworkers.*

DON'T SAY THIS: *"You need to start standing up for yourself"* or *"I warned you about taking that job!"* (Sending the wrong message: Your partner is incapable of solving problems or making decisions on his own.)

MISTAKE: It's an insult to your partner's abilities to offer blanket advice that's really a criticism. Launching a harsh "start-up" guarantees that he won't listen to you, because if he does, he'll be admitting incompetence. Always keep in mind that your partner made it this far in life without your advice, so imagining that he needs to stop and listen to you now is humiliating. Expect a severely negative Reactive Response.

ASK BEFORE GIVING ADVICE: Always get permission to discuss an issue—and set a time to do it. Not asking your partner if he wants or needs advice before giving it is disrespectful. In this case, you're both expressing doubt about his ability to figure things out on his own and telling him that he's weak for allowing people to treat him badly.

LONG-TERM RISK: Many times people only need a "sounding board," that is, someone who will listen without commenting. We all need to tell our stories, but won't risk telling them if we sense that our partner will be critical or accusatory. We'll just shut up . . . and bury our resentment about it. Not a good thing for any relationship's long-term health.

SAY THIS: Simply, *"Tell me about it"* or *"After you've told me the whole story, would you like to hear my perspective?"* (Sending the right message: I trust your ability to deal with the issue.)

WHY THIS WORKS: Asking for specific guidance about how to proceed is smart. Only venture where you're welcome. Always get permission before offering anything, from advice to a massage.

COMMIT TO LISTENING: The comment *"Tell me about it"* is neutral and requires only active listening—keeping constant eye contact and not allowing distractions to interrupt. Those are important, because if your attention wavers, the person speaking will likely feel that you don't care.

The second response, *"Would you like to hear my perspective,"* is trickier. Now you've signed on to do an even more intense form of active listening, because you need to digest all the facts before offering any ideas. Don't offer this option unless you're ready to fulfill it completely.

REAL-LIFE STORY: Bob didn't like talking with Jenny about his divorce five years ago. But before she would discuss getting married, she said she really wanted to know more about what had happened. During a long road trip, she gently prodded Bob to speak, and he slowly told her the complicated and painful story. Afterward she felt she knew him better and trusted him more.

Hey, Are You Horny?

THE SITUATION: *You've been thinking all day about sex with your part-ner, and when you get home, you get right to the point.*

DON'T SAY THIS: *"I'm feeling horny. Wanna have sex?"* (Sending the wrong mes-sage: I act like a selfish teenager when it comes to sex.)

MISTAKE: Not a great approach. Blunt requests for sex are risky for several rea-sons. First, you haven't taken time to sense your partner's mood—and might get a curt refusal. Becoming sexually aroused depends on feeling attraction in the moment. Second, if either party feels obligated, the result might well be a boring, discouraging and dispiriting sexual experience. No matter how horny you feel, this is not a wise way to say so.

SEX IS SITUATIONAL: You can't separate having the right conditions from enjoy-ing a good sexual connection. Countless books about sex—and vast amounts of research—demonstrate incontrovertibly that great sex requires the right sit-uation for both partners. There's a popular myth about two people being so excited and synchronized in their desire that they explode into mind-blowing sex on the kitchen floor. Sure, it can happen. Maybe. If all the conditions are perfect. But 99 percent of the time, sex is a longer process—one involving lov-ing consideration of your partner's needs and desires.

SAY THIS: *"Honey, I'd really like to spend some time together, maybe later tonight. Want to talk about it—while I'm giving you a massage?"* or *"Darn, you're looking sexy!"* (Sending the right message: I can be sensitive, charming and humorous.)

CHARM AND HUMOR ALWAYS WIN POINTS: Not enough can be said about the role of charm and humor in relationships. Charm is the power to delight and attract people. Humor is the ability to see the inherent comedy of a situation (not another person), especially one's own. Both qualities create a sense of lightness and fun. Research into successful relationships demonstrates that couples who bring levity and humor into their everyday interactions— especially ones as important as sex—report far greater satisfaction than those who don't.

HOW ABOUT FLOWERS? The value of a flowery (or any creative) gesture can be powerful. Use your imagination . . . not your domination.

BUILDING INTIMACY: Since sex is our most intimate (and emotionally risky) behavior, it naturally requires us to practice our greatest degree of sensitivity. Especially important is that we avoid saying or doing anything that could offend our partner and trigger a Reactive Response. So . . . go slowly and sensitively.

The Sex No Longer Sizzles

THE SITUATION: *You love sex with your partner, but one night he doesn't perform well—and you're both frustrated.*

DON'T SAY THIS *(sarcastically):* *"Well, wasn't that fabulous!"* (Sending the wrong message: I'll make you pay for disappointing me.)

AN IRONCLAD RULE: If there is *one* rule for couples about communication, it's this: Never use sarcasm as a way to express dissatisfaction or unhappiness.

SARCASM DESTROYS RELATIONSHIPS: Sarcasm is punitive and destructive. Using sarcasm forces the person hearing the words to reverse them to understand their actual meaning. Being forced to work to recognize the real intention behind a message and then tolerate that the message is negative and critical invariably creates resentment and anger.

A GUARANTEED BAD OUTCOME: The moment either partner in a relationship employs sarcasm, the focus will shift to the sarcasm itself, distracting from the real need: to improve the situation. And it may entirely destroy a couple's sex life.

KINDNESS IS IMPERATIVE: Dealing with sexual nonperformance, dissatisfaction or mismatches in tastes demands exquisite tact and sensitivity. A brusque, harsh or punitive message can have long-term negative effects on performance, especially for men. Any kind of significant stress inhibits the erectile response and will create frustration for both parties.

INSTEAD, SAY THIS: *"Honey, everything isn't always going to be perfect. What's important is our love for each other."* (Sending the right message: I know what's important between us.)

PUT LOVE AT THE CENTER: It's easy to forget that sex is known as "making love" for a good reason. While a certain amount of "performance" is always required—since we ask our bodies to do certain things—the most important reason for sexual intimacy within a committed relationship is to build our emotional connection to each other.

SHUN TOO MUCH SAMENESS: If either partner gets stuck in a specific sexual expectation or demand, that will create stress and work against the couple's long-term happiness.

AVOID PERFORMANCE ISSUES: Engaging in sex at different times of day and night can lower stress, reduce expectations and alleviate the stress of performance. The amount of time you dedicate to each other can vary greatly, from a "five-minute quickie" to an hours-long massage, surprising the body and delighting the senses.

GO FOR VARIETY: Because so many factors can affect sexual appetite and the ability to perform, couples need to have a variety of sexual activities satisfying for both partners. Playing fantasy roles, reversing common gender activities, taking turns with achieving orgasm, performing mutual masturbation and various forms of oral pleasuring are just a few of them.

Now let's shift from one-on-one relationships to the sometimes stressful, always challenging and frequently joyful arena of raising children, aka parenting.

PART THREE

Parenting: Don't Say That to Your Kid... Instead Say This

The relationship between parent and child is markedly different from any of the other relationships addressed in this book because there's an immense differential in power between parents and children.

Until children reach adolescence, parents possess almost all of the power. They make the decisions and the child goes along. Once children enter adolescence, of course, the power differential begins to equalize—as it must—until children enter adulthood, when parent and child begin to treat each other *almost* as equals.

Younger children are acutely aware of this power differential and do their best to cooperate in meeting their parents' needs and desires.

But serious problems arise when parents self-indulgently abuse their power. For instance, when a parent repeatedly speaks to a child contemptuously, employing any of the components of blame (criticism, accusation, punishment or humiliation), the cooperative and loving connection becomes frayed.

Most parents do this out of ignorance: They don't really know (or pay attention to) how critical, accusatory and humiliating words damage their children's trust in them. Worse, they're oblivious to how such attacks affect children's trust in themselves and their belief in themselves as valuable. Children who come to believe that they deserve humiliation will act from that unhappy place, sometimes for the rest of their lives. After all, children *cannot* protect themselves from absorbing their parents' negative messages.

So when Justin's father tells him that he's stupid and worthless—or lazy and selfish—he accepts those descriptions as true, at least unconsciously. When he next approaches a difficult task, his internal monologue will likely be, "Why bother trying? I'm stupid."

The reverse is true when parents *over*indulge. When Masie's parents are willing to do anything to keep her happy at every moment—no matter how unreasonable—Masie will naturally come to believe that the world revolves around her every whim.

Parents, of course, rarely go about consciously creating negative outcomes for their children. But tens of thousands of interactions occur during the decades of parenting, and enough thoughtless actions by parents are certain to negatively affect children's self-esteem.

On the other hand, the parent-child relationship is capable of producing more meaningful change than any other. The words you say as a mother or father or uncle or aunt or grandparent (or teacher) have a *profound* effect on the child. Often making subtle changes in how you speak to a child can make a significant difference in that child's life.

On that encouraging note, let's dive into some of the most typical scenes in parenting.

How Many Times Have I Told You . . . ?

THE SITUATION: *Your twelve-year-old son comes home from school, drops his backpack near the door and starts to play a video game.*

DON'T SAY THIS (angrily): *"I've told you a thousand times to put your stuff away before using the computer! Why are you so stubborn [lazy, difficult, stupid]?"* (Sending the wrong message: I must use anger to control your behavior because you're too difficult.)

IT WON'T HELP: Criticizing loudly and angrily may provoke a Reactive Response. Or your son might bury his reaction until it surfaces later in lack of cooperation. Neither helps establish discipline.

IMPARTING A BAD HABIT: Yelling angrily when your child does not comply is a product of thoughtlessness, of not thinking through the consequences of your actions. Even though your child might not be able to verbalize his feelings, he or she will be absorbing the message: Yell first, think later. So thoughtfulness is essential when setting limits.

DON'T ASK QUESTIONS THAT CAN'T BE ANSWERED: This is one of the Five Rules of Effective Communication (part of the book's introduction) that is especially crucial to parenting. After you've asked your unanswerable question, what's the next step? What answer could your son possibly come up with as to "why" he's so stubborn or difficult? How does tossing this "question" at him address the underlying issue—how you're going to control his overindulgence in video games? And even if he does submit and pick up his stuff, how will you deal with his sullen attitude? Those are the questions that actually need answers.

SAY THIS *(calmly)*: *"Justin, please follow the rules about putting your stuff away before doing anything else."* (Sending the right message: He has to follow the rules.)

RULES APPLY TO EVERYONE: One of the most important components of raising children successfully is establishing rules and principles that guide everyone in the family, including parents. Abundant research into successful families demonstrates that children feel less anxiety and perform better when parents clearly explain expectations and consequences—and no one in the family is exempt from the rules.

NO EXCEPTIONS: If children watch parents violating the family's standards, such as overindulging their emotions by yelling or losing their tempers while punishing children for those same behaviors, children's respect for the parents will decline and the family's overall happiness will deteriorate.

WHAT'S FAIR IN YOUR FAMILY?: Fairness is a core element of success. Parental hypocrisy on any level is highly destructive to family cohesiveness and undermines the child's success. So ask yourself: What code of conduct guides your family?

ORGANIZE YOUR FAMILY: Use Family Meetings (see the "Family Meetings Can Teach Everyone to Say the Right Thing" segment of the "Advanced Work" section at the end of this book) to set rules to which everyone agrees. Contrary to many parents' beliefs, children do not like anarchy. They respond positively, like all human beings do, to sensibly set limits and consequences for violating them.

This Homework's Too Hard

THE SITUATION: *Samantha's fifth-grade teachers have been complaining that she often turns in unfinished homework.*

DON'T SAY THIS: *"If you weren't so lazy and worked harder, you could easily finish it."* (Sending the wrong message: Your problems aren't real; there's something wrong with you.)

DISMISSAL DOES DAMAGE: This comment dismisses your daughter's feelings, minimizes any study problems she may have and will likely leave her feeling isolated and emotionally abandoned. Furthermore, after you've made this comment, what comes next? Since you've insinuated that she's simply lazy, she doesn't have many options. Your accusation has reinforced any negative views she might hold of herself and created a roadblock to her making further effort.

DON'T REINFORCE A NEGATIVE SELF-IMAGE: This injunction must be one of every parent's primary challenges. Just as a physician must first do no harm, so, too, parents must remind themselves *to not do or say* anything that harms the child. Name-calling is at the top of the list. Parenting's most constant task is to resist yielding to the first emotion that surfaces.

RESIST YOUR OWN REACTIVE RESPONSE: When parents see their children struggle, their first reaction is fear—that their child will not keep up with his or her peers and eventually fail. This fear triggers a Reactive Response in parents that can prompt them to attack the child. It's a primitive response and absolutely unhelpful—if not downright destructive.

SAY THIS: *"I can see this is difficult for you. Can I help in any way?"* (Sending the right message: I recognize your problem and will offer help—if you really need it.)

ACKNOWLEDGE THE PROBLEM: Accepting that in your child's mind she really *is* having a hard time avoids an argument over whether her problem is real. By asking her if there's some way you can help, you're inviting her to participate in finding a solution. She now has the task of figuring out whether you can help her. And if so, how.

POSITIVE MEANS EFFECTIVE: Since no child realistically enjoys going to school unprepared and getting a poor grade, your job is to help avoid the stress of that failure. If she fails, both of you will suffer. So your best strategy is to review your past interactions with her over study and homework issues and figure out what approaches have proved most effective.

ACHIEVING BALANCE: Successful parenting involves finding a balance between supportively helping the child and taking over and doing it yourself. This challenge is constant, and only becomes more difficult during adolescence. Children endlessly seek autonomy and independence yet are stuck in utter dependence. It's a balancing act, rarely easy for anyone—but achieving it enhances the entire family.

ACCESS YOUR RESOURCES: As an adult you have resources your child doesn't have. Who can you ask for help? Does your child need a tutor? Could a high school student help with homework? Use your resources.

He Started It!

THE SITUATION: *Two brothers, aged eleven and nine, blame each other every time they get into a fight.*

DON'T SAY THIS (*yelling*): *"Your fighting all the time is driving me crazy!"* (Sending the wrong message: I'm powerless to stop your fighting. Insanity is my punishment for being ineffectual.)

PRESERVING PARENTAL AUTHORITY: Don't abandon your parental authority by acting out your frustration and anxiety. You're the adult and know more than your children about how to live a successful life. Yelling to solve a problem between siblings obviously doesn't work, because you're joining the fray. The boys quickly learn that they need only get you worked up for your authority to disintegrate in a hail of ineffectual threats. It's a lose-lose situation for all involved.

KIDS WILL BE KIDS: But not every grown-up is an adult. Distraught and frustrated parents often display a lack of emotional maturity by giving in to their own Reactive Responses. Occasionally getting angry and yelling might not be a problem if it occurs very rarely. But it spells endless cycles of trouble if you use it regularly in an effort to set limits for children.

MORAL AUTHORITY IS PRECIOUS: Raising your voice in anger or frustration risks your losing moral authority as a parent. One of the greatest sources of authority for a parent is the modeling of morality. If a parent preaches self-control but regularly loses it, their attempts at discipline will be ignored. And from a child's level of logic, rightly so.

SAY THIS *(placing yourself between the fighting boys): "I want you boys to separate and take turns telling me what happened . . . calmly."* (Sending the right message: I can guide your behavior without using anger.)

ENGAGE CHILDREN'S INTELLECT: This tactic diverts attention away from angry physical acting-out and toward using words to express feelings . . . and needs. Talking about a problem involves the intellect (one hopes!) and is the absolute best way to teach children how to find solutions. Of course this kind of intervention takes time and energy. Parents must take this process seriously and make sure that their daily schedules allow time for thoughtful intervention.

SIBLING FIGHTING IS A PARENTING ISSUE: In many instances siblings can settle their own arguments and work out solutions by themselves. Conflicts involving excessive anger, physical violence, or one sibling overwhelmingly dominating another, however, require parental intervention. In these cases it is crucial that parents take responsibility for children's learning and assertively step in.

INTELLIGENT INTERVENTION: Intervening intelligently and thoughtfully is the winning strategy for any parent-child issue. The constant theme in all these scenes and situations is putting thinking first. The parent must ask (thoughtfully): *"What do I want to accomplish with this intervention?* (See the Five Rules of Effective Communication in the "How to Use This Book" section.) Always ask yourself: How can I intervene most intelligently?

She Cries to Get Attention

THE SITUATION: *Your nine-year-old daughter bursts into tears about going to school.*

DON'T SAY THIS: "You're only crying to get your way." (Sending the wrong message: I don't care about your tears.)

MISTAKE: Dismissing your child's feelings gives her the message that her emotional needs aren't valid. You're teaching her that "crying out for help" is not only futile, but that you're going to criticize her for it—which gives her the impression that there's something wrong with her for feeling sad or afraid—and accusing her of deliberately manipulating you. These are very serious acts of blame.

ASK RATHER THAN ASSUME: A constant theme in good parenting is to be moderate and balanced in your responses. Your daughter's tears are neither to be ignored nor a reason for you to collapse emotionally, or give in to her demands. What's clear is that she's deeply unhappy (in that moment) about the prospect of going to school. Why? Your job is to find out.

SHAMING CUTS DEEPLY: Fortunately children's feelings can change rapidly and they can quickly forget unpleasant events. But children do not forget being blamed and made to feel wrong. No matter how fleeting the criticism, all varieties of blame and shaming can burrow deep inside and form emotional scar tissue that builds up over time. This fact about human development must be part of every parent's wisdom.

SAY THIS: *"Sweetie, I can see you're upset about going to school. Can you tell me why?"* (Sending the right message: I care about your feelings and struggles.)

TALK ABOUT HER FEELINGS: Take a few minutes to "problem solve," to discuss what's going on. Usually, once your child expresses the real source of anxiety, you can find a solution together.

ACCEPTING ISN'T CAVING: Accepting that your child is upset and wanting to find out why does not mean that you have to give in and do whatever your child wants. If you did, your child would likely be doubly distressed. Seeing that you can easily be manipulated by negative emotion, her insecurity will actually increase. Children really don't want to be in charge. Yes, they want their way, but they also want parents strong enough to guide, nurture and protect them.

CHILDREN NEED LOVE: How do parents show authentic love for their children? It's more than cooking, cleaning and giving hugs—a hired nanny could do all that. What children need is love—understanding and acceptance—a definition of love that applies to every relationship, including friendship and marriage. Understanding means "I hear what is true for you" and acceptance means "I accept your feelings and beliefs as valid." When these two qualities are active in any relationship, the other person will feel loved. Children who are actively loved will prosper despite their fears and anxieties.

You're So Irresponsible!

THE SITUATION: *Your teenage daughter comes home two hours past curfew, and you're furious.*

DON'T SAY THIS (*yelling*): *"How could you be so irresponsible? You're grounded for the week. Give me your cell phone!"* (Sending the wrong message: I'm going to act out my anger by punishing you.)

MISTAKE: Since it's so late, you have a right to be worried, and even angry. But indulging your anger and issuing a draconian punishment is a mistake. If you do so, you're giving your daughter a false target: your angry reaction, triggered by your own Reactive Response. Once you interject strong negative emotions into any situation, those emotions will likely become the issue. Furthermore, the situation can quickly escalate into an all-out power struggle.

DEFINE YOUR GOAL: Of course it's natural to vent as soon as you see your daughter. But once you've exploded, then what? Consciously ask yourself: *What do you want to accomplish?* Your first task as a parent is to find out what happened; who and what caused her to be so late? If you confront her angrily and immediately impose a punishment your daughter will shut down and turn off. Or, unwilling to offer any substantial information that might further incriminate her, she'll blurt out a series of excuses and falsehoods. Neither teaches her anything about how to prosper in a complex world.

SAY THIS: *"Honey, I'm really angry right now. Go to bed and we'll talk tomorrow about the consequences."* (Sending the right message: I can control my emotions and focus on the issue.)

SMART MOVE: By remaining calm and deliberately delaying discussion until tomorrow, you're keeping the anxiety where it belongs—within the mind of your misbehaving daughter. What's Mom or Dad going to do? How serious will it be? How many restrictions will be imposed? By allowing her to wallow in these uncertainties until *you* are ready, you're controlling the agenda.

IT'S THE RELATIONSHIP THAT COUNTS: No parent can coerce a teenager into compliance if the teen truly doesn't want to comply. Kids are known to engage in superficial compliance coupled with secrecy. In extreme cases they'll run away and put their lives in danger rather than give in to a tyrant or abuser. So make sure that your actions are thoughtful and designed ultimately to bring you and your child closer together.

INTELLIGENT INTERVENTION: The thoughtful parent takes time to figure out the best way to intervene in order to accomplish his or her goal. And the primary goal is *always* to bring your child closer so that he or she will absorb your parental guidance and wisdom. To repeat: Meaningful teaching can happen only in the absence of anger and anxiety. Parental thoughtfulness is the primary source of meaningful teaching.

Should confrontations and problems occur frequently, the most effective method for solving them is to hold regular Family Meetings, as discussed in far greater detail in the "Advanced Work" section at the end of this book.

PART FOUR

Friendships: Voluntary Relationships That Make Life Better

We all admire people who have and maintain a group of lifelong friends.

In the vitally important interactions we call friendships, what you say and don't say makes all the difference between creating long-lasting bonds with people you like, and having people keep their distance.

Creating authentic friendships is not a superfluous issue. Abundant research demonstrates incontrovertibly that people who have a solid group of friends and share social time with them on a regular basis are significantly happier and healthier than those who don't. People with friends even live longer and suffer from fewer health problems.

Why would that be? The answer is logical: Life is inherently stressful, and talking about our lives or just being in the company of people we trust alleviates stress because we feel less alone, less vulnerable and more connected to life itself. In fact, the benefits of professional psychotherapy lie to a great degree in having someone with whom to discuss personal issues who listens carefully and is committed to our welfare.

And that's the best definition of a friend: someone who's committed to your welfare.

Friendship is an area where the Five Rules of Effective Communication are particularly valid, especially the first one: *Decide in advance what you want to accomplish.*

This rule might seem simple, yet it's profound. Asking yourself, "What do I want to accomplish?" before making a particular comment or committing a certain action will automatically avoid a majority of catastrophes, including having friendships go sour, dwindle away or disappear.

As previously noted, the guiding theme of *Say This, Not That* is to *always think in advance about what you want to accomplish*. This requires putting your brain before your body, your thinking before your emotions, in order to avoid saying something that will set off the dreaded RR—a Reactive Response. Observing and controlling your anger, resentment, frustration, irritation, anxiety, fretfulness and fear is crucial. Everything you do to monitor your potential to set off an RR will solidly contribute toward your greater happiness and fulfillment.

A NOTE ABOUT SOCIAL MEDIA: The emergence of online socializing means that we use the word *friend* more widely now than in former times (how many Facebook "friends" do you have?), and that puts us in yet more potential peril. Photos of your rowdy behavior at a party can instantly reach a dozen (or a hundred) people. Via phone or video, so can your comments. Every small action can now go—to borrow a term—viral.

In this world of omnipresent technology, how can you protect yourself and your friendships? Even more important: How can you defend your peace of mind?

Because the proliferation of social media can instantly amplify a snappy, brusque or even rude comment into a major international incident within hours, it's even more important to practice extreme care when sending messages to friends . . . about friends.

Always keep in mind the First Rule: *Decide in advance what you want to accomplish*. When the answer isn't immediately apparent, you definitely want—at the least—to do *no* harm.

I remember a patient named Marion who became furious when she discovered flirtatious e-mails her best friend had sent to her husband. How could her friend betray her that way? At a party that night, Marion, to everyone's shock, loudly and angrily confronted her friend. A week later, Marion brought the e-mails to therapy and asked me to read them. Yes, they could be *interpreted* as flirtatious, but not enough to justify creating a full-scale catastrophe. Unfortunately for Marion, many guests from the party now saw her as a bit unhinged, which Marion bitterly resented. "I'm the victim!" she insisted. Sadly, Marion had not worked out her strategy beforehand. She'd just reacted!

Contrast that with this story. Geoff pursued a long-standing dream of starting a small business. After a few months of successful operation, he learned that a casual friend had written a blog piece sarcastically criticizing it. Geoff's family and close friends were outraged. How could that person be so disloyal! They wanted Geoff to write a counter-article and concocted numerous methods for ostracizing his blogging friend from their social circle.

But Geoff consciously chose another way to deal with it. When he learned that his now former friend would be at a social gathering, he decided to attend, and rehearsed how he'd greet him. When they did meet, Geoff was consciously friendly, made no mention of the criticism, and if anyone brought it up, he'd just smile. Over the next few days several friends complimented him on his diplomacy, his ability to be "bigger than" the other person. His intentionally calm behavior won him much admiration.

Developing a conscious strategy to not react is entirely different from suffering in resentful silence, taking on the role of victim. Rather, it's thinking carefully about rule one: *Decide in advance what you want to accomplish.* And beyond that, it's thinking over how you want to be seen and thought of by your social and business circle—what kind of reputation you'd like to enjoy.

So let's look at friendship. The following scenes provide specific guidance about how to deal with tricky situations between people you *choose* to know: your cherished and valuable friends.

SCENE 44 *She's Just Too Busy to Call Back*

THE SITUATION: *You've left three messages for Liz and she hasn't called back. Finally, on your fourth attempt, you reach her.*

DON'T SAY THIS: *"Well, Liz, you're obviously too busy to return my calls!"* (Sending the wrong message: I will punish you for disappointing me.)

AN EXAMPLE OF DESTRUCTIVE COMMUNICATION: Your sarcasm is accusatory and punishing: two damaging components of blame. No one enjoys being punished, especially by a friend. Even if you get an apology, your friend won't forget your punishing comment. Human beings remember nasty behavior, and if you do it again in the future, your friend might give up . . . and disappear.

FRIENDSHIP MEANS EQUAL RESPONSIBILITY: You don't want to be the only one in a friendship who's putting in energy. If Liz is repeatedly difficult to contact, or you're the one who always has to initiate the connection, then you need to assess the benefits of trying to maintain a one-sided friendship. Even then, however, it's not emotionally healthy to criticize or accuse the other person. Simply accept her limitations (see page 215 on personal limitations) and devote your energy to someone who's both more available and who accepts the responsibilities inherent in longtime friendship. Just acknowledge the facts—without engaging in blame or condescension—and move on.

SAY THIS (*in a neutral tone of voice*): *"Hi, Liz. Glad to reach you. I can guess you've been busy."* (Sending the right message: I tolerate frustration and resist judgments.)

By not opening the conversation with a confrontation, you're giving Liz a chance to explain herself—if she chooses. Maybe she's been sick, or an emergency absorbed her attention. When you begin the conversation neutrally, you open the door to a simple heart-to-heart discussion of what's going on in your lives.

BE A GOOD FRIEND: When you don't use blame (criticism and accusation), you're demonstrating two of the core qualities of friendship: acceptance and understanding. After all, every one of us gets distracted and caught up in the whirlpool of our own life. It's often difficult to maintain our responsibilities to everyone we know. By not accusing Liz of being a "bad friend," you are being, in fact, a good friend. By definition you are acting like a person who cares about her welfare.

WHAT DO YOU WANT TO ACCOMPLISH? If you truly value your connection to your friend, you always want to strengthen the relationship. But even when you're unclear on what you want to accomplish, the goal of strengthening the relationship remains a constant. Even in casual interactions with people you don't know well, you want to expand your humanity and be your most friendly, generous and gracious self.

RELATIONSHIPS TEST US: Rarely does a friendship run smoothly all the time. It's when there's conflict that we're tested in our ability to be the best person we possibly can be.

My Friend Is Talking Behind My Back!

THE SITUATION: *You've heard that a friend has made negative comments about you.*

DON'T SAY THIS (angrily): *"Hey, what's this I hear about you saying crap about me?"* (Sending the wrong message: At the first hint that I've been wronged, I attack.)

MISTAKE: Before launching into a direct confrontation, ask yourself: How reliable is your source? Might the person spreading the story have an ulterior motive? Are there competitive forces at work? Could there be different interpretations of the conversation? Be an emotionally mature adult and consider all these factors *before* issuing an edict of condemnation.

ALWAYS AVOID ESCALATION: Once you have angrily confronted another person—even if you believe it's justified—it's very difficult to back down and smooth over the rift. Being verbally aggressive can create a far bigger problem than the original offense.

REAL-LIFE STORY: Terry attended a weekend party with several of his friends from work. On Monday morning a friend told him that another friend, Chuck, was telling people that Terry had been drunk at the party and had made passes at women. Terry was furious. He confronted Chuck, and within seconds both were shouting. Terry's boss heard about it, and because of that incident, Terry's promotion was canceled. Terry had painted himself as unsuited for greater responsibility within the company.

SAY THIS (*calmly*): *"Do you have a moment to talk about something I heard?"* (Sending the right message: I'm a reasonable person.)

USE A SOFT OPENING: Beginning a conversation (or an e-mail) with a "soft opening" (as opposed to a harsh one) helps avoid instantly triggering the other person's Reactive Response. After all, the person who you believe is saying something nasty may already be on edge, and hearing your voice (or message) might trigger an alarm.

ASK YOURSELF WHAT YOU WANT TO ACCOMPLISH: This first of the Five Rules of Effective Communication strongly applies here, because what you want to accomplish is definitely *not* to harm yourself. You do not want to needlessly alienate another person, negatively affect your reputation, or torpedo your friendship(s) or career. In this situation, Terry's approaching Chuck with a neutral question, soft facial expression, and relaxed posture allows Chuck to admit to telling some funny stories about the evening—one of them including Terry's having tripped and fallen into the arms of Chuck's girlfriend. He apologizes for making it sound like Terry was drunk. They part as better friends because neither had taken an accusatory position, which the other had to defend.

REMEMBER: MEMORIES ARE OFTEN DISTORTED. When researchers delve into memory and perception in an attempt to discover who really remembers what happened, they typically find that errors of memory can completely distort the facts. Keep this in mind before you consider confronting anyone about an event someone says he clearly recalls. Sometimes it's best to decide deliberately to do nothing.

She's Late Every Time!

THE SITUATION: *When it's your friend's turn to drive to work together, she always arrives late.*

DON'T SAY THIS *(angrily): "You're late again! Why can't you get here on time? Really!"* (Sending the wrong message: I'm going to punish you for being late.)

Directly confronting anyone's chronic lateness rarely if ever changes their behavior because deeper unconscious motivations are usually at work. If you need to remain dependent on a chronically late person, you must adopt a more effective strategy.

PERPETUAL LATENESS IS PASSIVE-AGGRESSIVE BEHAVIOR: Habitual lateness is often more than just bad time management. Along with its cousin, chronic procrastination, it usually conceals deeper emotional issues such as unconscious anger and resentment, which the passive-aggressive behavior helps to express, albeit dysfunctionally. Each time Jill arrives late, she apologies profusely. But if she were really sorry, she'd change her behavior.

In actual fact, she's subconsciously glorying in her ability to *displace* her *unacknowledged* anger onto her friend with little effort.

WHAT DOES THE LATECOMER GET OUT OF IT? For one thing, Jill has now gotten Anita to experience her *anger for her*—without doing anything overtly aggressive to set her off. She avoids being seen as the angry person, even to herself! For another, whenever Jill arrives late, whether to pick up Anita or for any other event, she's automatically the center of both attention and control. Quite an array of payoffs for simply dawdling.

SAY THIS (*firmly but calmly*): "*I can't afford to be late for work, so either you'll need to be here on time or I'll have to find another way to get there.*" (Sending the right message: I can take care of my own needs—and not play your game.)

THE POINT: Adults find their own solutions. They connect with people who are dependable.

IT'S ALWAYS ABOUT BOUNDARIES: Even though it might not seem so at first glance, this is also an issue of maintaining healthy physical boundaries. Jill has repeatedly invaded Anita's space by creating a problem; namely, violating her agreement to get Anita to work on time. The only solution when someone continually violates your boundaries is to take calm but firm action to stop the violation. Getting angry only plays into the drama and keeps the wheel of action-reaction-action-escalation going around and around.

IN REAL LIFE: Anita needs to follow through on her statement that she'll find another way to get to work, perhaps by organizing a carpool. Most likely Jill will react by blaming (criticizing and accusing) Anita for being too rigid, as though there's something wrong with Anita because she objects to delays. When passive-aggressives are called on their games, their suppressed anger often erupts to the surface.

There's no negotiating with authentic and chronic passive-aggressive behavior. The only strategy is to avoid any form of dependence.

They Broke Up and Now He's My Friend Again

THE SITUATION: *Your friend disappears for months at a time when he's dating someone new, then reappears when it's over and acts like nothing happened.*

DON'T SAY THIS: *"Well, I suppose you just got busy."* (Sending the wrong message: I'm a pushover and can't take care of myself.)

MISTAKE: An authentic friendship can thrive only when the emotional and physical exchange is fair and equitable. You need to confront him with your feeling that he needs your friendship only when he's run out of other options. If you don't, you'll reinforce your sense of exploitation and perhaps develop the belief that you don't deserve much from friends. You'll settle for crumbs.

TEACHING PEOPLE HOW TO TREAT US: It's tough to remember that we *teach* people how to treat us, but it's true. Why can't they always be respectful and considerate? Why doesn't your friend realize that it's unfair to ignore you each time he's pursuing a romance? Why? Because we are all self-indulgent and self-centered . . . at times.

YOUR JOB IN THIS SITUATION: You must teach your friend that such starkly selfish behavior is not okay with you. If you don't teach him to treat you better, you will, by default, allow this pattern to continue. He needs to know that when his behavior swings wildly, depending on who's paying attention to him, you lose respect for him as a person. Loss of respect produces permanent deterioration in friendships.

SAY THIS: *"I really want to continue our friendship, but I'm not willing to be a friend only at your convenience."* (Sending the right message: I recognize my needs and I'm willing to take care of them.)

IT TAKES COURAGE: Confronting a friend with the truth about what you will and won't tolerate takes emotional strength—in a word, courage. Suppose your friend gets angry? Suppose he storms out? It's not easy.

COURAGE IS CRUCIAL TO GOOD RELATIONSHIPS: Being courageous is not usually considered part of forming and maintaining relationships. Yet life is littered with examples of times when you should have acted but hesitated. The bottom line is constant: If you don't stand up for yourself, who will? And if not now, when?

REAL-LIFE STORY: Franklin and Sean have been friends since college. Recently Franklin left for a monthlong vacation with his new girlfriend, Allyson, and after his return took another month before responding to Sean's e-mails and messages. Franklin finally contacted him and they met for coffee. Sean told Franklin that during his absence his brother had been in a serious car accident; he'd really needed a friend to talk to and was angry and disappointed that Franklin hadn't responded. Franklin instantly apologized and admitted to being so distracted by his new love that he hadn't even read the e-mails. "I've been a real jerk," he said. "And what's weird is that Allyson probably ended up dumping me because I'm so damn self-centered. I think it's time I grew up."

How Come You Don't . . . ?

THE SITUATION: *You've known Jessica since grade school, but you're finding her constant critical comments about your life to be painful.*

DON'T SAY THIS: Nothing! Just be endlessly patient, hoping someday she'll get it. (Sending the wrong message: I'm a victim.)

REAL-LIFE STORY: When Jessica comes to visit, her eyes scan your living room and the comments begin. "You're still living with that bright color?" And, "I love your table . . . the 'funky' look!" She laughs as though she doesn't mean it. Inside you're simmering. Her unwitting criticisms go on. "You have such patience to stay with Judd. I mean, really." More laughter. You can't wait until she leaves.

But you've known Jessica forever and can't just dump her. She's been loyal. So when Judd comes home you complain to him. He says, "I'm really tired of hearing about how Jessica is always dissing you." Now you feel doubly isolated, angry with both your friend and your boyfriend.

A HISTORY OF CRITICISM? Sometimes relationships have a built-in "pecking order" in which one person persistently teases or degrades another. Siblings are famous for this: The older sibling assumes the right to dominate or persecute the younger.

SAY THIS: *"Jessica, you must stop making your critical comments about my life and way of living. If you don't, I'll have to stop seeing you."* (Sending the right message: I choose to have only supportive people as friends.)

ARRANGING TO HAVE A HEART-TO-HEART: It's best to set up a time to talk about an issue that's sensitive and could have life-changing consequences. So when you arrange to meet at a neutral setting (a café), state firmly but respectfully exactly which behaviors she must change. Use clear examples of what bothers you. Tell her firmly that you no longer want to hear so-called humorous comments that are actually criticisms.

HOW SHE MIGHT RESPOND: Be prepared for an initial shock, perhaps even an explosion. But also be ready for a possible confession of guilt and a compassionate plea for forgiveness. Often, a heartfelt and fairly conducted confrontation can yield a flowering of authenticity and genuine feelings of remorse, followed by increased affection.

FRIENDSHIPS ARE VOLUNTARY: Once you're an adult, there's no reason to tolerate ongoing and persistent emotional abuse in *any* relationship. Self-care requires that you protect yourself from anyone who doesn't respect you, your tastes or your lifestyle. And you *can* protect yourself.

THE MEANING OF FRIENDSHIP: If you're going to spend time with a stranger and establish an ongoing connection—a friendship—you must trust that your friend will respect your physical person, your occupation, way of life or sexual orientation, and even your tastes. Life's problems never cease, so being able to appreciate the absurd and chuckle along with friends at your foibles is important. But that's different from letting them subject you to constant mockery.

PART FIVE

Say This . . . in the Workplace

Your employment, occupation, job or vocation—where you work to make money to survive—can be the most difficult and stressful of all environments in terms of interpersonal communication. You're spending time with people who, in most cases, you have no other relationship to other than work. The focus is goal-oriented and productive: creating a product or providing a service in order to earn a profit for your company or organization. As for your personal stake at work: Your efforts earn you money and status, which combine to ensure your future.

Succeeding at work *requires* you to interact productively and professionally with others. There is little room for emotional outbursts or fits of anger in the workplace. In fact, how effectively you interact with others can mean the difference between prospering or failing, between happiness and despair. So there's a lot at stake even when you exchange a few casual words over coffee.

The most immediate approach to making sure that your communications at work are constructive is to focus on *always* practicing healthy boundaries.

Here's a quick review of how healthy boundaries function, both *physical* and *emotional*.

Your physical boundary is the space around your body: how close you get physically to others and how close you allow them to get to you.

This includes your sexual boundaries. You'd typically consider a light touch on the shoulder accompanied by a simple smile to be innocent and friendly. But add a leering, sexually charged smile and . . . whoa! Your sexual boundary has just been violated even when no further touch is attempted. The suggestion *alone* constitutes a violation. Likewise, telling a sexually tinged joke can violate boundaries.

Emotional boundaries are more difficult to define. Your history, what kind of family you grew up in and your overall level of emotional maturity will all strongly influence not only how you act but—most important—how you *interpret* other people's emotions and behaviors.

Being conscious of your *interpretations* is the key to having healthy emotional boundaries.

If Becky, for example, with whom you'd shared a glass of wine and a lively conversation just a few days ago, arrives at the office and barely nods, you could interpret her behavior in different ways.

If you have healthy emotional boundaries, Becky's behavior will bounce off the protective shield they provide. You'll make a mental note to talk to her later and get on with your work.

On the other hand, if you have weak, porous or unhealthy emotional boundaries, you might spend your entire morning upset and brooding. "Why is she acting that way? What did I do?" And when you meet her later, you might act from that place of emotional injury and say something offensive—making matters worse. This is why boundaries matter so much.

In the example with Becky, there are several different ways you might react to her rushing past you at work with hardly a nod—and they differ, depending on the strength of your emotional boundaries.

But there's also a more profound way to look at her behavior—as well as the behavior of every other person with whom you have contact—your parents, siblings, partner, spouse, children, friends and coworkers—and that's to understand the Law of Personal Limitations. Here it is:

Everyone is always doing as well as they can within their personal limitations, their personal history, what they know and don't know and what they're feeling in that moment. If they could make a healthier decision, they would. This includes you.

At first glance this might seem to suggest that you adopt the permissive attitude that "anything goes." But in fact the law requires *thoughtful* and *compassionate* responses to other people's actions. The thoughtful part demands that you think about the best way to react . . . and try to take a compassionate view of other people's behaviors.

This law is profound in its consequences and influences. These three sentences encompass insights from both the great philosophical and religious traditions of past millennia as well as from solid psychological research.

In fact, the Law of Personal Limitations (LPL) is utterly logical and withstands every challenge (for a more detailed discussion of the law, refer to my book *Beyond Blame*, published by Tarcher/Penguin).

Let's take the simple example of why Becky ignored you that morning, but from Becky's point of view. The night before she'd learned that her sister and her husband had filed for bankruptcy, and would lose their business, have to sell their house and move far away. Becky hardly slept, woke up with a headache and arrived at work besieged by a host of Personal Limitations: emotional, physical and financial. These barely allowed her to notice you. Her family's life had just spiraled downward. Talk about personal limitations!

Yes, it would have been better for you had she summoned the energy to say, "I just got some terrible news and I'm really upset; let's talk later." But another of Becky's personal limitations is that when she's troubled, she doesn't reach out. Her approach is different from yours—when you're troubled, you can't stop talking. Which your friends understand and kindly tolerate.

Now, it might sound simplistic to insist that everyone is inevitably restricted by personal limitations. But, in fact, few of us ever consider how powerfully personal limitations affect everyone. Most important, we rarely acknowledge these limitations *before* we blast someone (or ourselves) with criticism, accusation, punishment or humiliation.

In the following scenes, we'll explore responses to situations at work from both the perspective of the Five Rules of Effective Communication (choosing the most helpful words) and the Law of Personal Limitations (searching for deeper understanding). Both approaches provide depth and breadth to all the scenes in this book.

I'm Perfect—Why Aren't You?

THE SITUATION: *You start work early and stay late to get your assignments done before deadline—and your coworkers aren't pulling their weight.*

DON'T SAY THIS: *"You know, if everyone did their job around here, some of us (me!) could have some time off."* (Sending the wrong message: I'm so much better than everyone else.)

HUGE MISTAKE: Talk about losing friends and allies! You're not only criticizing other people's performance, you're accusing them of having a weak work ethic. Your accusation will alienate just about everyone including your boss, and you'll be judged to be an inadequate team player.

APPLYING THE LAW OF PERSONAL LIMITATIONS: Everyone has limited emotional and physical resources. Some of yours might be: (1) You can work twelve-hour days, but intermittently burn out and need to hibernate; (2) you might be highly organized but short on creativity, and (3) you might be intensely loyal, but your lack of tolerance for those with less passion may be seen as fanaticism.

So accusing other people of being slackers because they don't measure up to your standards (which also come with limitations) will only sabotage your career in the long term. From a practical point of view, having compassion for people's differences better serves your own core needs and best long-term interests.

SAY THIS *(to yourself)*: *"People can only do the best they can in any given moment. We all need to lead balanced lives. I must keep in mind my long-term goals and not be too extreme."* (Sending the right message: I practice self-awareness and moderation.)

Moderation and balance are the constant themes throughout this book. Pushing yourself too hard and then being critical of others for not measuring up are examples of immoderate behavior. Being overly harsh with either yourself or others for not being able to accomplish every task on every possible occasion ignores the Law of Personal Limitations.

LECTURING YOURSELF IS A PROVEN TECHNIQUE. Talking to yourself about what's most vital to your success and long-term happiness is a verified way of staying balanced. Giving yourself positive messages is good, but it's also important to focus your thoughts on what's ultimately important.

A SAD REAL-LIFE STORY: Maeve would set out her clothes every night to make sure they matched perfectly, and arrive at work every day a half hour early, fully prepared. She would memorize staff meeting notes and never hold back in telling colleagues when they'd missed something. Her reputation for arrogance concerning her efficiency irritated the hell out of everyone. No one ever asked Maeve to join them for lunch or drinks, and her social isolation began to deeply trouble her. One day, after being hospitalized for panic attacks, she was let go on the grounds of emotional disability. She had "outperformed" herself into joblessness.

It's Not Me—It's Them!

THE SITUATION: *You couldn't finish a task on time and your supervisor confronts you.*

DON'T SAY THIS: *"Well, the jerks in the other department screwed up!"* (Sending the wrong message: I'm unable to take responsibility for my own part in the failure to get this job done.)

MISTAKE: Getting defensive, self-protective and accusatory is a very bad response because it reveals emotional immaturity. And diverting the discussion into other subjects compromises your reputation as reliable.

DEVELOP A STRATEGY: No environment is more personally treacherous and unforgiving than work. Your lifetime goals involving success and financial reward are at stake. An emotional outburst or an inappropriate response can instantly jeopardize your future, and rarely do you get a second or third chance to rebuild your reputation. What you say and how you behave make all the difference between advancement and stagnation—or even simply staying employed. For these reasons, it's essential to have in place a strategy to control your Reactive Responses.

NAME-CALLING IS DANGEROUS: Diverting responsibility onto someone else is always difficult and tricky, but calling another person or group disparaging names labels you as untrustworthy. After all, who calls other people names? Children. Being seen as childish—as immature—means you're not up to the job . . . and certainly not a candidate for a position involving increased responsibility.

SAY THIS (*softly*): *"I'm sorry the project's late. Do you have a moment to talk about what happened?"* (Sending the right message: I recognize the problem and want to discuss it.)

ACCEPT RESPONSIBILITY ONLY FOR YOUR PART: Acknowledging that the task has fallen behind schedule shows that you're not denying the facts. The second sentence indicates that you also aren't accepting full responsibility. In two brief sentences you've engaged your supervisor in examining the problem and yet not exposed yourself fully to the consequences. Above all, your even tone of voice implies you are confident in your ability to reach a resolution.

MODERATION FIRST: With the exception of (occasional) energetic friendliness, which might translate as enthusiasm for the job, high emotion in a work environment drains energy and diverts attention. The job is the job, and how you feel about it is mostly irrelevant. If every coworker insisted on expressing his or her emotional state regarding every issue, a lot of time every day would go solely to dealing with everyone's feelings.

SELF-CONTROL IS KEY: The ability to control your anxieties concerning an error or delay allows coworkers and supervisors to trust your responses. This translates over time into willingness to grant you more responsibility. The most successful employees and executives are those who remain calm even in highly stressful situations. Other people are naturally attracted to those qualities of maturity and self-control.

How Come Nobody Told Me?

THE SITUATION: *You learn that a meeting involving your colleagues took place without you.*

DON'T SAY THIS (*peevishly*): *"Why didn't anyone tell me? Why am I being kept in the dark?"* (Sending the wrong message: I'm easily distressed when I think I'm being ignored.)

MISTAKE: There might be several reasons why you weren't told about the meeting. Maybe its topic was not your specialty or responsibility. Indulging in petulant questions, irritated tone and accusations of conspiracy all put you in a lose-lose situation. First, people now have to deal with your irritation, which consumes time and emotional energy. Second, they now have to take time to answer your accusation. Finally, if you were left out of the communication loop on purpose, your primary task is to find out why. And find out in a more professional way. Emotional confrontations are not professional.

WHOM CAN YOU TRUST? In order to get accurate information about how and why you didn't learn or weren't told about the meeting, you'll need to talk to someone you trust, and few people trust those who are accusatory and threatening. Alliances at work are based on trust, mutual need and sometimes on affection. But when a person's livelihood and career are at stake, alliances can shift rapidly. Accusations will drive people away and leave you isolated.

DON'T ROCK THE BOAT: This applies to most work situations. It means not creating waves that sink the boat that everyone depends upon to keep from drowning. Be patient, stay calm and take your time figuring things out.

SAY THIS (*giving solid eye contact*): *"I'm really sorry I missed the meeting. Somehow the message never got to me."* (Sending the right message: I'm a professional who can deal with problems.)

LIFE IS COMPLEX AND MISTAKES HAPPEN. The most effective strategy is to treat your misinformation as an accident. Be patient and more will be revealed. Maybe someone is actually out to sabotage your position. If so, you'll need your wits about you. Playing it cool is the best strategy because you're not alerting anyone to your suspicions. This is a win-win position because if it was a simple mistake, no big deal, and if something else is going on, you're positioned to figure it out.

STRATEGY IS IMPORTANT: Strategy means that you have a plan, a path toward accomplishment. Being strategic means not just creating a mess by giving in to your Reactive Response, but instead, patiently weighing your options. Armies train soldiers to stay calm when under attack because a frantic warrior is useless. The same advice applies to advancing your career: Stay calm and levelheaded. Don't flap around like a squawking duck. Rather, glide like a swan; pad softly like a cat. Act so that you retain others' respect for you. And take action only when you're truly ready.

She's Nitpicking My Work

THE SITUATION: *You've just started working with a new procedure and your colleague is criticizing your performance.*

DON'T SAY THIS: *"You know, Jan, I'm smart enough to figure this out. Get off my back."* (Sending the wrong message: When I feel wounded, I strike back in return.)

MISTAKE: Reacting strongly to feedback, whether negative or positive, is not the sign of an accomplished professional. The true pro doesn't get overly excited about either failure or success. After all, there are countless minor battles. And who's to know if, in any particular moment, pushing for a "victory" is really in your long-term best interest.

EXCITABILITY IS SCARY: Your coworkers will treat anyone who's overly excitable with wariness. But by far the worst behavior is interpreting negative feedback as a personal attack, and responding with aggressive defenses. Doing so is especially risky in professional settings.

REAL-LIFE STORY: Marc opened a consulting firm with his colleague Bruce. All went well until Marc realized that Bruce completed reports without including important data. When he spoke to Bruce about the problem, Bruce denounced their new hires and even implied that Marc himself was to blame. Bruce's defensiveness became chronic and eventually Marc had to dissolve the company in order to disassociate himself from Bruce's personal issues.

SAY THIS *(in an even voice)*: *"Thanks for the feedback. Can I look it over and get back to you tomorrow?"* (Sending the right message: I'm available to correct my mistakes.)

EXCELLENT STRATEGY: Your response accomplishes three things at once. Your composure demonstrates that you're not upset by possibly having made a mistake. Your requesting time to review your work gives you and others an opportunity to determine whether you need to self-correct. And finally, in citing a specific time (tomorrow), you're committing yourself to a deadline for review. All of these demonstrate a high level of maturity and professionalism.

A STORY OF PROFESSIONAL SUCCESS: Yolanda knew she had a lot to learn when she joined an established company. She was determined to absorb lessons from everyone, even subordinates. Whenever someone offered her advice or information, she made sure to maintain unwavering eye contact and keep her expression neutral, and finished by thanking the person for his or her advice. When she knew she might be wrong about something, she immediately consulted with a colleague. Consequently she developed an excellent reputation—a typical comment being "Yolanda's great to work with." She rose rapidly within the firm.

He's Really Got It in for Me

THE SITUATION: *A coworker makes constant sarcastic comments about your character and competence.*

DON'T SAY THIS *(angrily)*: *"Mark, you'd better cut the crap you're saying about me . . . or else."* (Sending the wrong message: I'm easily offended and respond with threats.)

MISTAKE: Direct confrontation escalates situations by feeding negative energy with more negativity. Mark now can justifiably focus on your confrontational snarling rather than on his own disparaging comments: "I barely said anything and he just exploded!" Even if Mark is expressing his own insecurity by trying to pull you down, you don't want to give him more fuel for his accusations.

BE STRATEGIC: Some people are bullies. They have a nasty streak inside and they vent their nastiness by finding victims and systematically denigrating and belittling them. A bully in the workplace is dangerous to your career and must be dealt with thoughtfully and strategically. It's essential to develop a strategy to undermine their ability to harm you. *Most important is never to show bullies that their attacks are wounding you.* Just as sharks are attracted to blood in the water, bullies get excited seeing that their attacks are drawing emotional blood. Stay calm, at least outwardly.

SAY THIS: *"Mark, it seems like you have some issues with me. Let's discuss your concerns with a supervisor."* (Sending the right message: I think strategically so you can't outmaneuver me.)

GREAT MOVE! The last thing bullies expect is to have their tactics exposed to scrutiny. Bullies operate surreptitiously. They attack using only a small stiletto: The blade may not reach your heart, but can sap your blood. You have a variety of ways to defend yourself, the most powerful being the threat of open discussion. This strategy only works, though, when you present it coolly and as an ordinary part of business negotiations.

IN THE NAME OF EFFICIENCY: Your goal in discussing Mark's criticisms with a superior is to enhance your company's efficiency—not to get revenge. If Mark is incorrect in negatively assessing your performance, you want to dispel his ignorance. If there's some truth to his critiques, and you need to make positive changes, you're demonstrating a willingness to make them. At no time act defensively. Everyone you work with needs to see your attempts at self-improvement and dedication to the company clearly.

TEAM PLAYER: Companies thrive when everyone works together. Anything you do to enhance your perception of being a "team player" will advance your career.

I've Got All the Answers

THE SITUATION: *You notice a colleague is not following correct procedure.*

DON'T SAY THIS: *"Here, let me show you the right way to do that"* (loudly, so all can hear). (Sending the wrong message: I know everything and will prove it.)

TRIPLE MISTAKE: The first mistake in this response is that nobody likes a know-it-all. Flagrantly exhibiting your knowledge is simply an adolescent form of "showing off" and always creates resentment. The second mistake is offering advice without asking permission. Unless there's an emergency and adhering to correct procedure is crucial, it's disrespectful to barge in and tell others they're wrong. The third mistake is arrogance: claiming that you and only you know the "right" way. Are you absolutely positive? Are there extenuating circumstances you don't yet know about, such as a special request from the boss involving this particular task? Take a few seconds to ask permission thoughtfully before volunteering a correction, and avoid offering information unless you're certain.

AVOID HUMILIATION: While outperforming one's colleagues might create resentment, it rarely breeds desire to seek revenge. After all, merit is generally respected. But humiliating another person is different. Humiliation creates enemies. Never humiliate a colleague or supervisor.

SAY THIS *(in a congenial tone)*: *"Would it be okay for me to offer a sugges-tion?"* (Sending the right message: I'm sensitive to your situation and can be diplomatic.)

A WINNER: Diplomacy and timing are everything in communication, especially in work environments where power and status are directly connected to suc-cess or failure. The phrase "Would it be okay . . ." asks permission and implies respect for the other person's position. The words . . . *for me to offer a sugges-tion* convey a neutral position. All you're offering is a suggestion, not claiming to possess ultimate knowledge or demonstrating how superior you are to the other person. You're not saying anyone is wrong.

USE NEUTRAL, NONEMOTIONAL PHRASES: The constant theme in these scenes is selecting words that convey a neutral, nonemotional attitude. The goal is to avoid triggering a Reactive Response. If your words, facial expression or body language convey disapproval or blame, you'll have to deal with the other per-son's anger, resentment or anxiety. These negative emotions make every inter-action more difficult.

REAL-LIFE STORY: Latoya has a wonderful and welcoming smile and uses it to smooth over her interactions with her subordinates. When she has to correct an error or give a subordinate some critical feedback, she makes sure to begin the conversation with her bright smile, which puts the other person at ease. Her words are soft yet she's also known for not being evasive or mushy. After the intervention, she smiles again and assumes a supportive tone. The result is that Latoya has built a solid reputation as an effective manager.

PART SIX

Everyday Situations

E veryday encounters, whether with a neighbor or a stranger, can make a big difference in your day, your week . . . or even your life.

You never know when something you say—or don't say—in a chance encounter may create a moment of peace and harmony, or end in disaster.

The most effective guideline for such times is found in the basic message of this book: Take a few seconds to think about the most effective way to reply. Above all, do everything possible to avoid provoking a Reactive Response, both in yourself and in the other person.

This can be difficult at times, because these encounters are spontaneous. While the first two scenes in this section (an intrusive neighbor and a chronically complaining relative) are fairly common, the other two present the challenge of thinking quickly and clearly and responding precisely.

Here's a classic example: Doug is leaving a restaurant with his girlfriend. Two men entering the restaurant make a comment about women, which Doug hears as being offensive to his girlfriend. A quick glance at the two men tells him that they've probably been drinking. Giving them any kind of response might result in a disastrous escalation. So

Doug takes his girlfriend's arm and they walk away, averting a potential blowup.

All the scenes, though, point toward the same approach: Take care of yourself and respond strategically—in a way that advances your best long-term interests.

The Intrusive Neighbor

THE SITUATION: *Your neighbor accosts you at every chance he gets to offer advice about everything and gossip about everyone.*

DON'T SAY THIS: *"You know, Fred, I really don't need your advice. And I don't appreciate hearing gossip."* (Sending the wrong message: I react belligerently—beware.)

MISTAKE: Even though you really don't need or want advice or gossip from Fred, aggressively telling him to stop will not help create neighborly feelings. Neighbors can be very important people in your life. Sure, you might not choose a neighbor to be your friend, but—important to note—unless you or they move elsewhere, you're stuck with them. In some instances, your relationship with your neighbor will last longer than that with a sibling.

AXIOM: NEVER CREATE NEEDLESS ANTAGONISM. This axiom runs parallel to "do no harm." You don't want to make Fred—or anyone—into an enemy. If you insult Fred, his neurotic and invasive energy might turn into the need to punish, and his focus then turn toward making your life miserable. So striving to avoid mutual hostility is entirely practical.

DEALING WITH SOMEONE'S PERSONAL LIMITATIONS: Fred is limited (as are we all) by his personality and background. These factors are beyond your control. He might also suffer from social isolation. Regardless, handling him calls for a two-pronged strategic campaign. One is to try to redirect his attention to something or someone else. The other is to blunt his attempts at contact with polite but firm refusals.

SAY THIS *(in a neutral tone of voice)*: *"Fred, I know you have a lot of information to share and I'm really sorry, but (a) I only have a few minutes to chat right now, or (b) I've got something else to do and don't have time to chat."* Repeat as often as necessary. (Sending the right message: I recognize your need and can refuse respectfully.)

KEEPING AN APPROPRIATE DISTANCE: Knowing how to stay engaged without being taken advantage of is a skill that can require practice. Although an invasive neighbor might seem fairly benign, dealing with him can become complex. Every opportunity to develop your skills is another chance to learn.

ADULTS CAN SAY NO: One of the simplest and yet most important functions of healthy boundaries is the ability to say no without explaining yourself. It's a sign of porous, poorly functioning emotional boundaries when you believe you have to explain your motives and justify your refusal. Except with your spouse or partner (who does need to know why you are deciding something), *you don't have to explain anything*! Saying no to Fred is just part of being an autonomous adult. "Sorry, Fred, but I don't have time to chat." That's all you need to say.

WORK ON YOUR OWN LIMITATIONS: If you have exceptional difficulty saying no, you need to work on that limitation. It might be a longtime habit, but ultimately, it's self-imposed. You *can* change it.

For more on dealing with people's limitations (including your own), see the segment "The Law of Personal Limitations" in the "Advanced Work" section at the end of this book.

The Perpetual Complainer

THE SITUATION: *Your relative is constantly complaining about everyone and everything.*

DON'T SAY THIS: *"I've really had it with you and your negativity! If you can't say anything positive, I'd rather hear nothing."* (Sending the wrong message: I have neither patience nor compassion.)

TOO HARSH: Your words convey one basic message: Stop, and stop right now! While this might succeed in the short term, it's far too harsh to serve your long-term interests. In fact, it's humiliation—a component of blame. It's humiliating because your words bluntly inform this person that there's no value to anything she says, so she herself has no value to you as a person. The likely result? A Reactive Response. And all the complications and escalations likely to follow.

TACTICAL ERROR: Your relative's Reactive Response will now cause her to focus on you. You've given her reason to divert her attention away from the content of your request and focus on your being mean and unfeeling. Sadly, she'd be correct in doing so. Lose-lose.

SAY THIS: *"Betty, I know you're having a tough time . . . and you are often very critical. Can we talk about this?"* (Sending the right message: I can see you're in pain and I'm willing to discuss the issue.)

A DIFFICULT MOVE: Not an easy response for anyone to give, but one that's necessary. You're telling her that because you value your relationship, you're willing to take a risk and tell her that you're not happy with what she's saying. You'd like her to make some changes. Your invitation to discuss the issue also tells her that you care enough to engage on a deeper level.

HOW TO DISCUSS THE ISSUE: A good approach is to use the guidelines of Constructive Conflict. First, get permission to have the discussion—which sets up an expectation of "serious" communication. Focus on your message and what you want to see happen! You could say: *"Betty, I know that you often feel overwhelmed. But I can't hear only about your problems. You need to blend in some more positive things, too. Does that make sense?"*

BE READY FOR FAILURE: No matter what you say, no matter how patient and compassionate you might be, your relative may remain negative. Her attitude may be too deeply etched into her personality for her to change. At which point you might have to defend yourself further by saying, *"I love and care about you, but I just can't handle so much negativity. It's too much for me. It has to stop."* This message is both caring and firm.

He's Always Interrupting

THE SITUATION: *Your friend always comments about everything and won't stop interrupting.*

DON'T SAY THIS: *"Will you just shut up and let someone else talk! You're so self-centered!"* (Sending the wrong message: My frustration forces me to be rude and insulting.)

IT'S A COMMON PROBLEM: There's always going to be someone we know who has poor communication skills. If the way this person talks or acts is a chronic problem, you'd probably just stop seeing him and the friendship would shrivel up. But sometimes life requires you to stay in contact with the person (you may have a work, family or community connection) and you'll have to find a way to communicate your needs—without destroying the relationship.

DON'T JUST SUFFER: On the other hand, it's not fair to yourself to just suffer in silence and get irritated and frustrated every time you're around this person. Inevitably your discomfort will push you to do or say things that create a crisis or reflect badly on you. And telling yourself that there's nothing you can do other than endure being bored or offended doesn't sharpen your own communication skill in stating what you need.

SAY THIS (TO YOUR FRIEND): *"When you have a moment, I'd like to talk to you about something important."* (Sending the right message: I can use my advanced communication skills to work on an important issue.)

FIRST ASK PERMISSION: When you have a few minutes of quiet time together, tell your friend: *"I really care about our relationship, and I want to give you some feedback about how you communicate. Do you want to hear it?"* Most likely you'll get back an anxious answer. Wait until your friend agrees to listen before offering advice.

THEN SAY: *"You are probably not aware of it, but I must tell you that you interrupt and talk over just about everything I say. I'd like you to be aware of your impatience and simply slow down."* If this advice is received in a reasonable way, you can then go on to discuss more about the issue. You might even suggest the simple exercise of counting to five before talking. But the bottom line is that the constant interruptions really have to stop.

A COMPASSIONATE INTERVENTION: All too often people aren't capable of dealing with an important issue in a positive, supportive and compassionate way. Inviting your friend to talk about your concern—and giving direct feedback— shows that you care enough to address the issue with compassion.

FIRM AND DIRECT IS BEST: Research shows that people really want to hear advice and suggestions, but they must be offered with respect and delivered in a caring manner.

I Can't Fulfill All Your Dreams

THE SITUATION: *You find yourself being constantly disappointed by friends, lovers, family members, politicians—the whole damn world!*

DON'T SAY THIS: *"You and your family and everybody else I know can go to hell!"* (Sending the wrong message to yourself!)

BITTERNESS AND CYNICISM ARE NOT OPTIONS: It's always easy to accuse other people of being manipulative, selfish, immature, dishonest, materialistic and on and on—all of which you yourself are *not*! But being cynical, pessimistic and bitter about people, society, social institutions, politics and life itself is an easy way out. Yes, it provides protection from disappointment, but also guarantees it.

DON'T FEED THE MONSTER: Generic negativity feeds on itself and can only yield greater bitterness and social isolation. Being disconnected from other people and society is a very unhealthy way to live.

EXPECTATIONS RULE OUR LIVES: Expecting people to be selfish will produce an unhappy outcome. A far healthier attitude is to be realistic. Memorize this: Everyone is constricted by a vast array of personal limitations, including you.

EMBRACE REALITY: Adjust your expectations to include the fact that you *will* experience minor errors, casual forgetfulness and trivial episodes of selfishness with every one you meet, because *every* human being is intrinsically flawed.

SAY THIS (*to yourself*): *"I'll be happier and have healthier relationships if my expectations are realistic and compassionate."* (Sending the right message: I'm reasonable and not judgmental about other people.)

MODERATION IS ALWAYS KEY: The ongoing theme throughout this book is the necessity of moderation in all things—including moderation itself. Which means that every now and then you can allow yourself to be extravagant. But rarely. And thoughtfully.

INCLUDING IN EXPECTATIONS: Moderating your expectations is also key—because expecting your friend, sweetheart, partner, lover, spouse or colleague to fulfill your needs at all times is irrational and will only lead to cynicism and unhappiness.

REAL-LIFE STORY: When Judd married Anita, he expected her to take care of the house while he made most of the money. Anita expected Judd to respect her job with a nonprofit even though she earned less than he did. Then she expected Judd to do his share of the shopping, cooking and laundry. They squabbled over these issues for a year. Before they could come to a resolution, they had to explore in depth their ideas and assumptions about gender roles and contemporary society, in which gender no longer defines specific jobs.

Adjusting your expectations and assumptions makes all the difference between having constant frustration and achieving inner peace.

When You Must Say Something

THE SITUATION: *Your best friend's husband comes on to you sexually.*

DON'T SAY THIS: Don't say nothing. Don't stay silent and just avoid him forever onward. (Negative message to yourself: I'm not worth protecting.)

SAYING NOTHING IS A MISTAKE: When someone perpetrates an assault or emotional injury against you, you might be tempted to say nothing. You don't want to make a scene (or hurt someone's feelings, get someone in trouble or break up a marriage), so you avoid taking action to defend yourself. But in these cases, defending yourself is a top priority.

FAILING TO BEAR WITNESS: When you're the victim of a violation and don't react, days or even years later you might still be asking yourself, "Why didn't I say something?" This can burn in your mind and every time you think about it you feel bad about yourself. Soon you might even blame yourself, thinking of yourself as a coward or a weakling. Or you wall it off in your mind so you never think about it. You find yourself avoiding the perpetrator, twisting your life around to make sure you never meet. All of these thoughts, feelings and behaviors pose significant and long-lasting danger to your emotional health.

A VICTIM OF YOUR OWN REACTIVE RESPONSE: When shocked by an assault or other invasive act, your body can easily go though its own RR, which shuts down your thinking. You can fail to protect yourself. Only later (sometimes much later) will your thoughts clear up enough to realize what you should have done. If that's the case, don't blame yourself for inaction. Instead, learn from the experience.

INSTEAD, DO THIS: Immediately get away from the perpetrator, grab a friend or close relative and tell him or her what happened. Be explicit. Use your outrage at being sexually assaulted (because that's what it is) to declare that you won't tolerate it. If you make a scene, so what? *You* are the victim. Like many perpetrators, he's probably counting on your silence, your being too embarrassed to blow his cover. Let him know *immediately* that he made a big mistake. (Sending the right message: I can take care of myself—above all.)

SELF-CARE IS THE ISSUE: Taking care of yourself is a profound and sometimes complex issue. True self-care goes well beyond achieving material success. It also requires saying and doing things that nurture your spirit, protecting your ethical standards and standing up for justice. All of which serve to advance your long-term happiness and fulfillment.

SELF-CARE TAKES COURAGE: Doing the right thing to take care of yourself occasionally means doing something that makes you uncomfortable. In some extreme cases it can cause problems for other people (like your friend's husband) as well as yourself. Yet it's the right thing to do, because doing nothing not only fails to protect you, but also goes against your ethics and beliefs. You *know* what's right. Trust yourself!

When There's Nothing to Say

MULTIPLE SITUATIONS THAT SHARE THE SAME DYNAMIC: *A stranger insults you on the street. A driver cuts you off. Someone posts a nasty comment on your Facebook page. You read a distressing article about a cruel event in the world.*

DON'T DO THIS: Don't get upset to the point of sleeplessness. Don't foolishly take unwise actions. Don't allow yourself to become cynical and antisocial. (Sending the wrong message: Random events control my actions and happiness.)

INSTEAD, DO THIS: Incorporate into your daily life this enduring philosophy shared by many beliefs and religions that's elegantly encapsulated in the Serenity Prayer:

Grant me the serenity to accept the things I cannot change,
the courage to change the things I can,
and the wisdom to know the difference.

How does this fit into the preceding scenes?

The consistent themes of *Say This, Not That* are thoughtfulness and strategic thinking. Thinking strategically always involves asking the single question: What do I want to accomplish—for my long-term best interests? Not for immediate gratification, or a self-indulgent impulse to get even, but long-term interests.

And, considering one's best interests, there are many instances when doing nothing—responding with an "enlightened shrug"—is the best strategy.

It's best to ignore the stranger who throws out an insult. Anyone crass enough to insult a stranger is possibly a dangerous person. Ignoring him is the wisest course.

Disregarding the driver who cuts you off is wise. Once you're certain that the other driver is not a danger, take a few slow breaths and keep your distance. It's not your job to teach other people how to drive. And if he's driving aggressively, stay out of his way! An attempt to get his attention could put you in danger.

Someone posting a negative comment on your Facebook page is more complicated, but your response needs to be similar. Sure, you'd like to explain yourself, or get even, and probably have the right to. Strategically, though, it's usually a mistake because you're literally adding fuel to the fire, inviting an escalating round of conflict, and perhaps encouraging a professional bully.

The best approach to these types of situations comes by way of one of my professors in psychology who taught from the Jungian perspective of archetypes: Act as though you're the monarch—the king or queen—and therefore are above the petty nattering of the ignorant. It's a useful image, and helps keep you from being swept along by the mob.

So many times during any given week I scroll the Serenity Prayer in front of my eyes and remind myself to take some slow, deep breaths and think about how powerless I am to change so many things in the world. Amazingly, I find great solace in this message. Then, once I've slowed down my breathing and am able to calm my thinking, I focus on what I truly can change.

Which is, in fact, a lot. Every one of our decisions can be improved; everything we say can usually be said more expertly, thoughtfully and—especially—lovingly.

That is why I wrote this book.

Advanced Work

The compact format of *Say This, Not That* focuses on quick and effective solutions to problems in everyday communication.

But underlying these situations are many complex psychological dynamics. Even our simple behaviors are driven by processes too intricate to discuss in the very brief format of *Say This, Not That*.

This section presents an opportunity to learn more about these processes. Let's begin with the most fundamental of all, the concept of meeting one's Core Needs.

Core Needs

During the past twenty-five years of work with individuals and couples, I've found that one problem keeps surfacing—bobbing to the surface like a log—namely, that *many people neglect or even refuse to take care of their most basic needs.*

Take, for example, Nathan and Miriam. They have two school-age children. Miriam has just filed for divorce, and Nathan is shocked and angry. Sure, they'd had problems, but divorce? He wants to get even, to make her pay, so he hires a bulldog attorney and starts pouring money into the legal battle like it's a blood sport.

The kids, of course, are already frantic from all the tension. When I confront Nathan with the fact that his desire for "revenge" is adding to his children's already significant trauma, Nathan completely ignores it. He's determined to make Miriam's life hell.

"But, Nathan," I continue to protest, "Miriam is the mother of your children. Any stress you cause her directly affects your children, whom you profess to love with all your heart. Hurting Miriam is directly against your children's welfare—*your* best long-term interests!"

Nathan doesn't care. Five or ten years later, his children will surely get even with him, but right now, Nathan has donned full metallic body armor and is impervious to the sword of reason.

Simply put, Nathan is, in his determined fury, refusing to take care of his Core Needs.

A Core Need is something that *you need to achieve happiness in the long term*. They're necessities that are *essential* to:

- advance your long-term best interests
- develop your character and personal integrity
- realize your deepest, most authentic self

THOUGHTS AND CORE NEEDS

How can your thoughts help or hinder you in meeting your Core Needs? Simple: Thinking can create anxiety and prompt behavior.

If you *think* (or believe) that the driver who just pulled in front of you must be punished, your subsequent behavior could result in a fatal car crash.

If you *think* that your boyfriend is flirting with someone, your anxiety might keep you awake at night and result in a lousy day at work, or appear to justify a hostile confrontation that could torpedo your relationship.

In both of these cases, your thoughts may be based on erroneous assumptions. Therefore, they're not congruent with your long-term best interests. And therefore they interfere with meeting your Core Needs.

EMOTIONS AND CORE NEEDS

Most of our decisions are direct extensions of our feelings. Emotions can be our enemies, especially extreme ones. Fear drives us to fight or run away. Joy or romantic love can push us to make hasty and perilous decisions. Many of our strongest emotions work against us meeting our Core Needs.

Your Core Need in every relationship is to develop a heartfelt mutual connection and build a life together.

MEETING YOUR CORE NEEDS: AN EXAMPLE

Your best friend is giving you a party, and your fiancée arrives with her irritating and somewhat parasitic brother. You think, She knows that I don't like the guy—she must be bringing him to spite me.

But why would she do that? You go outside to give yourself some time to think, decide to rise above your annoyance, and return inside and welcome him. Your fiancée thanks you.

You've met a Core Need—*to be understanding toward your fiancée* and her complicated family situation. She's grateful for your maturity. You both feel closer.

Healthy Boundaries: Part of Your Core Needs

If there's a single need that's indispensable for success in all relationships, it's the need for healthy, functional *boundaries*.

In psychology, the term *boundary* describes the level of connection between two people and the *intensity* of their interaction. Typically, your boundaries can be described as healthy when you're neither too close to another person (over-involved and invasive) nor too distant and uncaring. Moderation is the absolute gold standard.

Boundaries exist in two basic forms: external and internal. Your overall emotional and even physical health depends on whether both forms of your "boundary system" are functioning well.

Let's first review your external boundary system. Take note, however, that because we're dealing with complex psychological processes (which affect everyone) there is usually some overlap between the external and internal.

EXTERNAL PHYSICAL BOUNDARIES

Physical boundaries refer to the actual physical distance between two people. If you're my sweetheart, spouse, young child or really good friend—and we have a mutual agreement—it will be fine for me to give you a hug, touch your arm or even give you a smooch. If we're not on good terms, however—even if we're married—these behaviors may be unwelcome, and touching in these ways would be a "violation of physical boundaries."

Do you know people who constantly get too close when they're talking to you? Or are overly affectionate and touch you in a way that feels uncomfortable? These people have problems with basic physical boundaries.

Sexual boundaries are a version of physical boundaries, but they involve every aspect of sexuality. We expect people to maintain the "social agreement" to not do or say something that involves unwanted sexual content. Certain words, gestures or a leering look can be sexual boundary violations.

INTERNAL EMOTIONAL BOUNDARIES

An internal boundary is your ability to protect yourself from being invaded by other people's feelings, needs and ideas. Healthy internal boundaries also restrain you from emotionally invading others.

When meeting someone new (i.e., a potential sexual partner and mate), a healthy and strong *internal* boundary helps keep you from becoming entirely absorbed in that other person's world. It acts like an emotional filter, protecting you from being overwhelmed by a fantasy world we often imagine to be "love," in which you imagine that all your needs for closeness will forevermore be fulfilled.

This same boundary also protects you from being (excessively) hurt by other people's self-serving agendas. Conversely, it holds you back from projecting your own emotions onto them.

Spiritual and philosophical boundaries describe the need to have your own spiritual and philosophical beliefs and not be criticized or coerced into ideas or behaviors that don't fit your needs.

Emotional boundaries involve many powerful emotions that energize our daily life, but basically they *protect me from your emotions while still allowing me to recognize them*. I must be strong enough emotionally not to be consumed by your personal drama. If you're feeling down about something, I still must be able to go on with my plans and not feel as down as you do. At the same time, if your sadness, pain or anxieties leave me entirely unaffected, then I've constructed an emotional wall, rather than a boundary.

If either you or another person compromise this "boundary system," the relationship will suffer.

Here's an example of how internal emotional boundaries work. You see your partner looking glum and your own mood takes a dive. This means that your emotional boundaries are too weak because you have immediately allowed your partner's feelings to take over your own.

Or let's say that you meet Julie for a few dates, fall head over heels in love, imagine that she will love you forever and tell all your friends that you've met your soul mate. Your emotional boundaries have collapsed. When your fantasies fall apart, will you blame Julie for not being loving, or do the correct thing and hold yourself responsible?

WHAT HEALTHY BOUNDARIES TELL US

We can describe the thoughts in a healthy boundary system this way:

"I have a right to my own thoughts, feelings and beliefs, and you have a right to yours. I'm not responsible for your emotional life and needs, nor are you responsible for mine. We will take our time to see where we do agree and where we don't, and will respectfully negotiate any issues that arise between us."

At first reading, this description may sound a bit hard-hitting. Indeed, it usually requires some thought and study to get to the truth embedded in its words. But I can guarantee that the time you'll spend thinking about it will prove worthwhile.

THE BENEFITS OF STRONG BOUNDARIES

Building a healthy boundary system yields the following positive results:

ONE: You'll be able to tolerate your own anxiety and not allow it to push you into making life-changing decisions. You won't say yes to things that work against your own best interests.

TWO: You'll more easily tolerate other people's anxiety or pain when you need to slow them down—or stop something going on between you and them altogether.

THREE: You won't invade other people's spaces and create stress in your relationships. That's important, because stressful relationships don't last—or if they do, they create chronic unhappiness.

A positive outcome of developing a healthy boundary system, and better tolerating your own anxiety, is that you won't rush too quickly into anything. From buying a new computer or a new car to beginning a new relationship. You won't propose marriage after the third date. You won't say yes to things beyond your comfort zone. Healthy boundaries, in short, help you stay in control of your life.

BOUNDARIES AT WORK

Examples of dysfunctional and functional *emotional* boundaries:

THE SITUATION: As you leave a room, several people behind you start to laugh. You imagine they're laughing at you and suddenly you feel intense shame. "What's wrong with me?" you wonder. In fact, they're laughing at a joke that had nothing to do with you. But you've *allowed* the feeling of ridicule to penetrate your heart.

A functional emotional boundary would allow you to *think* about the situation and realize that you did nothing wrong. Their laughter would pass right by you.

THE SITUATION: You find out that a good friend held a birthday party and didn't invite you. You're upset and stew about it for days. Your dysfunctional emotional boundary allows the pain to overwhelm you.

But with a functional boundary system, you would call your friend and ask about her birthday. She might tell you that her sister had arrived unexpectedly and that they'd ended up holding only a private family gathering. Because you haven't allowed yourself to prejudge the situation, you get information that explains what had happened, and avoid suffering needlessly.

In these situations, a dysfunctional emotional boundary allows emotions to overwhelm your thinking, with negative results, while a well-established boundary system allows you to go on to the day's next event with your self-esteem intact.

Dealing With Anger in Relationships

Let's discuss the most destructive emotion in all relationships: anger.

It's anger that most often destructively disrupts our ability to meet our Core Needs and tends to defeat and break through boundaries, leading to negative results.

Anger has many forms: resentment, upset, annoyance, irritation, frustration and, in extreme cases, fury and rage. It can even explode, rather quickly, into violence.

Anger is our most dangerous and misunderstood emotion. It's misunderstood because most people believe that if they're feeling anger or any of its versions, they have the "right" to those feelings. And therefore they have a right to attack some other person for those feelings using criticism, accusation, punishment and humiliation—the four components of blame.

Not true!

Here's an example. You invite a friend to a dinner party and she simply doesn't show up. You're really upset (a variation of anger)—how could she be so inconsiderate? You plan to get even, to criticize her for being disrespectful and accuse her of being selfish.

But the next day you learn that the day of your party she'd had a car accident. Amazingly, your anger dissipates and now you're concerned for her welfare.

What about her blowing you off? That was only your perception, your belief, your *interpretation* of the limited information available at the time.

And that's common. Because typically, the power behind *excessive* anger is an inclination to judge everyone too severely—*including oneself*. The appropriate (and healthiest) response to most provocations is a ripple of irritation.

Because life is filled with mistakes, forgetfulness, misunderstandings, disappointments and missed opportunities, scaling back excessive anger—not allowing it to overwhelm your basic equilibrium—is essential for long-term happiness.

REAL-LIFE ADVENTURES WITH ANGER

THE SITUATION: You're excited about meeting your girlfriend for dinner after work and telling her about your promotion. The minutes tick by, and after waiting for half an hour—with no phone call—you're severely annoyed and leave the restaurant. Just outside the door she rushes up to you and apologizes profusely; she'd been stuck in a conference with her boss. Your body is still charged with anger, but you know she doesn't make up stories and want to forgive her. So you take a moment before responding, and during that moment realize that her delay due to work has nothing to do with her appreciation of you. After a few breaths you go back inside together and celebrate your good news.

THE SITUATION: You tell your boyfriend that you and your girl-friends are getting together to celebrate your birthday, and you expect that he'll get you something special. When he barely remembers to wish you "happy birthday" and doesn't even get you a card (much less flowers or a gift), you feel really angry. After a nasty argument, he explains that because his parents divorced when he was young and he had five siblings, birthday celebrations were nearly nonexistent. He hardly even remembers his own birthday. You both end up agreeing to coach him on the issue.

THE SITUATION: You receive a notice about a late charge on a credit card and yet you're certain you wrote the check. Furious at the credit card company, you call and accuse them of deliberately losing your check so they can charge a fee. But the next day you find the unmailed envelope wedged in the seat of your car. Now you're furious at yourself. Finally, you realize that all this anger is wasted and destructive energy. You made a mistake. Big deal. Next time you'll be more careful when mailing your bills. Lesson learned.

PLEASE, STOP! A Proven Method to Stop Escalating Arguments

Suppose that anger does break through, boundaries collapse and an argument erupts that escalates into name-calling and threats. What then?

In such cases you need an emergency method for *instantly* stopping the conflict before it escalates even further.

The basic premise of this method is that when either person's Reactive Response gets triggered, blood pressure and pulse rate accelerate, adrenaline floods the system and the ability to think clearly is severely compromised. Attempting to discuss an issue and reach a productive conclusion is *impossible* when either person is highly agitated and unable to think clearly.

Therefore, we all need a method to immediately stop escalation.

Now, this method can work *only* when all parties agree to respect its very simple single rule:

Either party can ask the other person to "Please, stop!" at any time, for any reason, without any need to justify their demand. The other person must immediately stop talking and also refrain from making threatening sounds or gestures.

That's it. Once either person declares "Please, stop!" everyone involved takes some time for their bodies to return to normal, at which time (an hour or a day later) they resume talking to each other.

The most common objection to this approach is: "If Eric could stop me from talking whenever he felt like it, we'd never discuss anything!" But if that's really the case, you and Eric don't really have a healthy, fulfilling relationship. You're adversaries, not partners.

My experience in working with hundreds of sets of partners is that when they have this method in place, it's rare that either abuses it. On the contrary: Knowing that either can stop an argument from escalating gives both partners a higher level of trust.

And if the issue is fundamentally contentions (i.e., your brother-in-law wants to move into your spare bedroom), the couple can use the problem-solving technique of Constructive Conflict to work through it.

Constructive Conflict: How to Resolve Problems in a Relationship

There are times when no matter how much people love or value each other, they will find themselves becoming volatile—or even hostile—when repeatedly discussing a particular problem.

The best way to fix this problem is to have a method in place, in advance, for dealing with difficult issues, a method that helps reach a relatively quick, peaceful resolution.

I have used the method described below with clients for many years and have found it to be the absolute best process for resolving conflict.

The process is called Constructive Conflict, and consists of four steps.

CONSTRUCTIVE CONFLICT: THE FOUR STEPS

STEP ONE: Choose a time when both of you are sufficiently rested (for instance, in the morning when you're fresh, rather than right before going to sleep). Turn off all media and phones. The process requires fifteen to twenty minutes.

STEP TWO: One person takes two minutes to state the problem from his or her point of view. Use a timer to avoid watching the clock. (You can agree to increase the time to three or four minutes if that works better.) The other person listens respectfully, *without interrupting*. When the timer rings, the other person takes his or her turn. Alternate this process for ten to twelve minutes.

STEP THREE: If the two people are sufficiently in control of their emotions (neither actively involved in a Reactive Response), they then use the remaining minutes to decide on a reasonable compromise. If, however, either party is too agitated to reach an agreement, they separate, and pledge to repeat the process within a day or so.

Important: After the session is over, neither person is allowed to casually talk about the issue without first asking directly for permission. "Do you mind if we talk about something you said?" It's perfectly fine to say, "No, let's wait until we're using the Constructive Conflict process."

STEP FOUR: Write down whatever agreement you make. Also write down whatever progress each of you has made toward understanding the other's position, in order to avoid later disputes over what was said or agreed to.

CONSTRUCTIVE CONFLICT IN ACTION

When conflict is managed respectfully, it can help bring people closer together. The following two cases demonstrate how this can happen.

CASE ONE

Jim has long played the role of therapist and peacekeeper in his extended family. Bryce resents that Jim's family calls anytime they're in crisis. Panicked phone calls frequently interrupt their dinners. Bryce withdraws into angry silence and Jim feels guilty. When Bryce gets to the point of leaving, Jim suggests a session of Constructive Conflict.

STEP ONE: They schedule their session for Sunday morning, when they'll both be rested.

STEP TWO: They flip a coin and Bryce takes two minutes to describe how he feels—namely, abandoned every time Jim jumps to respond to his family's demands. "It never stops! I cease to exist whenever the phone rings!" Hearing Bryce's passion, Jim becomes agitated. He shoots back, "Just because you grew up treated like a little prince . . . !" and stalks out of the room. The next day Bryce suggests another attempt. Jim explains his conundrum. "I feel trapped. On one side is my demanding family. On the other are my commitments to you." Bryce agrees that Jim is in a difficult place. His show of compassion softens Jim's position. Bryce says, "All I'm asking for is that during dinner, or when we go out—no phone calls. Just that."

STEP THREE: Jim agrees that Bryce's request is reasonable. "It won't be easy. I've trained my family to believe they own me. But I know that has to change."

STEP FOUR: Their agreement is simple, but it requires steady effort. When Jim slips up, Bryce disciplines himself to avoid fuming and withdrawing. Over the next few months Jim works to create better physical and emotional boundaries with his family. Because Bryce feels less resentful, he actively listens to Jim's issues. They feel much closer because now Jim's family is a problem they both share and work on together.

After several Constructive Conflict sessions, Jim realizes he has to put his family's needs second. He sets up limited and specific times when he's available to speak with them. Both he and Bryce then work to reinforce these essential limits . . . and emotional boundaries.

CASE TWO

Robin and Jeff have been together for two years and are beginning to plan their wedding. Robin manages a restaurant and teaches dancing, has hundreds of friends and wants a big wedding. Jeff, an accountant in a bank, wants to save money so that they can eventually buy a home. When he learns that Robin intends to borrow $20,000 to pay for their wedding, Jeff has a fit. Their discussion quickly escalates into a fight filled with accusations.

But because they are deeply devoted to each other, they decide to schedule an entire weekend to resolving their dispute. And rather than using the briefer version of Constructive Conflict (allowing twenty minutes for the entire process), they schedule several hours. Each person has a full ten minutes to speak while the other respectfully listens, and then they reverse roles.

Robin describes her lifelong dream of enjoying a fancy wedding and her family's tradition of putting on extravagant feasts. She had expected her family to pay for it but a financial setback is forcing her to finance it herself. Jeff narrates his history of growing up in a divorced family and never having any extra money; he's terrified of debt and financial insecurity.

After hours of listening to each other's stories without interruption, each feels much more compassion for the other's view. After the first sessions, they allow a week to pass before reconvening. Now, with a deeper understanding of each other, they negotiate a solution. Robin agrees to hold the wedding and reception at a friend's house and have family members contribute food. This brings the total cost down to $8,000, which Jeff easily agrees to.

This story of Robin and Jeff illustrates that even seemingly intractable disputes can be resolved when both parties dedicate themselves to reaching an understanding based on mutual respect.

Just as Constructive Conflict is an important method for resolving conflict between partners, Family Meetings are a vitally useful tool for everyone in the family to fulfill their needs.

Family Meetings Can Teach Everyone to Say the Right Thing

The purpose of the Family Meeting is to teach parents and children to work together to solve problems—and in the process, develop ethical, social and decision-making skills.

Family Meetings provide multiple benefits. The process of openly discussing issues and listening respectfully to every family member's ideas and feelings helps create a supportive environment. And all family members tend to accept more readily the resolutions and agreements that result because they're not just arbitrary pronouncements or edicts.

Family Meetings also help interrupt cycles of blame—criticism, accusation, punishment and humiliation. Minimizing these negative behaviors helps bypass the all too common cycles of revenge that tempt people of all ages when they're subjected to punishments they perceive as unfair.

Of course, decisions made in meetings will still include *consequences* for willful mistakes. But when the consequences are logical, fair and proportional to the seriousness of the mistakes, blame and retribution tend to dissipate.

These benefits, in turn, help build family closeness and trust.

Who constitutes a family? One parent and one child, two parents and multiple children or blended parents and children. All are families. Of course, the more individuals involved, the larger the combination of personalities—which will require more structure and perseverance to make the meetings work.

Crucial to making Family Meetings succeed is remembering the core characteristics of children, namely:

A. Children possess an innate sense of justice. They instantly recognize unfairness. They're sensitive to unfairness between siblings (or classmates), and always aware of double standards on the part of caregivers and parents.

B. Children possess intuitive abilities to constructively solve problems and are deeply invested in the success of the family.

C. Children are very willing to learn and cooperate—but require nonjudgmental guidance and a nonblaming attitude by parents.

You'll need at least three regularly scheduled meetings (one every week) to establish the meeting format, teach children the basic participation procedures, and allow some time between meetings to assure that everyone sees some visible results.

GUIDELINES FOR RUNNING A FAMILY MEETING

STEP ONE: Prior to the first meeting and each one that follows, parents place a notebook in a common area in which anyone can write (or have a parent write) an agenda item. Agenda items can be anything a family member wants. Obviously, certain issues or extreme requests are not open for discussion: use of violence, ethical violations such as stealing or lying, or legal violations such as children cutting school or using drugs or alcohol. These are valid subjects for a parental declaration. Otherwise, every agenda item is treated as valid.

STEP TWO: The parents choose a relatively unhurried time when everyone will be present. Sunday mornings or early afternoons often work best. A well-structured meeting requires approximately thirty to forty-five minutes.

STEP THREE: At the first meeting, a parent leads the family in choosing a chairperson and in deciding how often they'll rotate the position to a new family member.

STEP FOUR: As the meeting starts, the chairperson calls on every family member to give a simple compliment to each person present. Initially this may be difficult, but after some practice it can become a precious part of the family's week.

STEP FIVE: Each person who's written an issue in the notebook begins discussing it, taking about a minute to present the problem, followed by a statement of what he or she wants to see happen. Then other family members have several minutes each to express their views. The chairperson uses a timer to keep track of how many minutes each is using. Using time limits teaches the skill of staying on task. Respectful language is *always* required.

STEP SIX: The chairperson asks everyone to volunteer an idea or solution. If the family reaches a solution or compromise, it's recorded in the notebook. If there's no voluntary resolution, then the family votes on what should happen. Serious items requiring ongoing attention (such as disrespectful language, violence, vandalism, bad grades, alcohol use, etc.) are carried over for follow-up in future meetings.

STEP SEVEN: The meeting ends with a special family dessert or other treat.

HERE'S THE CONTROVERSIAL PART: *Every family member has an equal vote.* The younger children may need some guidance and a bit more time than others to think things through before they vote, but their voices must be heard. Parents often have difficulty accepting this because it's time-consuming dealing with children's opinions or resistance. Experience shows, however, that even the most stubborn child will want the meetings to work. Younger children eventually develop the skill of thinking through their ideas and describing them clearly. Counting each vote brings everyone into the discussion and allows for siblings and parents to build consensus.

A FAMILY MEETING IN ACTION

Jeremy and Vera have an eleven-year-old son, Finn, and a fourteen-year-old daughter, Maya. Their daughter's grades have been slipping and tensions between the siblings have been escalating. Vera is becoming distraught and blames Jeremy for being insufficiently involved. The whole family is becoming increasingly unhappy.

When their parents first call for a family meeting, Finn and Maya both sneer. Fortunately, the parents fully agree on holding a meeting, and insist that both children attend.

The meeting begins with Vera complimenting Jeremy for being there, and Jeremy tells his wife that she's a loving mother. The children refuse to compliment anyone.

The notebook Vera placed on the hallway table for agenda items lists Vera's worries about Maya's grades, the children's fights, and a request that Jeremy come home earlier from work. Jeremy hasn't written any agenda items. Maya has written, "Stop Finn from being a pest." Finn has circled Maya's name and simply scrawled "butthead."

Both Vera and Jeremy have promised not to react angrily to anything their kids say. Vera, the appointed chairperson, asks Maya to come up with some solutions for her falling grades. To both parents' surprise, she breaks into tears and blames the rest of the family members for making her life miserable. Her parents listen calmly—a big change from their usual frantic reactions. The meeting ends without written solutions, but to their parents' surprise, both children agree to attend the next meeting.

The next week's meeting begins in a cheerier mood since the children now realize that it isn't just a disguised forum for assigning them blame.

Jeremy and Vera (Mom and Dad) lead off with compliments to their children, and both Maya and Finn manage to mumble begrudging semi-compliments to each other.

Then come the written agenda items. Maya has requested to spend the weekend with a girlfriend and an increase in allowance. Finn wants another video game and less homework. Jeremy wants a date night out with Vera, and for Maya to stay at home with Finn so they won't have to pay a babysitter. Vera mentions her ongoing worries about Maya's grades.

Discussion of these agenda items goes on for nearly an hour. Maya agrees she'll try harder at school. She resists a more specific plan but seems less anxious. Afterward, Vera is astounded at how well the children worked together.

It takes several more meetings for them all to realize that discussing what they want, and suggesting solutions to their problems, actually works; that they're getting something positive for their efforts. It becomes part of their daily language to say, "Write it in the notebook and we'll deal with it at our next meeting."

A major breakthrough takes place when Maya scores an A on a test. To Vera's further surprise, her husband brings up the idea of a family vacation. By now, the family's new habit of working together to reach compromises on what they want—without excessive bickering—makes it easy to put together vacation plans. After several months of meetings, the family's overall level of satisfaction has greatly increased.

These principles of successful family meetings are really a miniature version of how a well-functioning democratic government works. That is, when everyone feels that they have something to contribute and their ideas are respected, their desire to participate constructively in society increases. Dissent is respectful and ultimately collaborative. The citizens prosper and peace reigns.

The Law of Personal Limitations: How Understanding Personal Limitations Can Affect Everything You Think, Say and Do

The topic of personal limitation was briefly discussed in the section on work. However the "law" is so vital to understanding the complexity of human interactions that it requires further exploration.

I describe the "law" as working on your Ph.D. in communication. It is literally a quantum leap ahead in understanding how and why every person with whom we have contact—parents, siblings, partner, spouse, children, coworkers and friends—says certain words or reacts in a particular way. Even more important is how understanding the "law" will help you comprehend *your own* behaviors and motivations.

"The Law of Personal Limitations" states:

People always do as well as they can within their personal limitations, their personal history, what they know and don't know and what they're feeling in that moment. If they could make healthier decisions, they would. This includes you.

(For a more detailed discussion, refer to my previous book *Beyond Blame*, published by Tarcher/Penguin.)

The most common objection to the "law" is that it seems to suggest a permissive attitude of "anything goes." It definitely does not. It does, however, require that you become more *thoughtful* about another person's (and your own) responses. It demands that you think about the best way to react, and not just follow your first impulse.

Let's take a typical situation to demonstrate how the "law" can apply.

You're planning a dinner party and you say to your partner, "I also invited Barrie. He's always fun to have around." Your partner frowns and says, "Not Barrie! He such an arrogant snob!"

You like Barrie's intellect and admit he can be sarcastic at times, but you've always overlooked his acerbic wit. Your partner says, "Last time he made a snide comment about my work. Who the hell does he think he is to talk to me that way?"

What's going on here? Is your partner overly sensitive? Is his reaction valid? Does this mean you can never invite Barrie to a social gathering with your partner?

In fact, you and your partner are operating within the range of your personal limitations. You grew up in a raucous family where everybody teased each other a lot, so Barrie's banter sounds normal. Your partner's family was more staid and formal, and Barrie's comments would be seen as offensive.

Neither family is "wrong." But the patterns show how growing up creates specific "limitations" that can lead to a lack of understanding, and flexibility about attitudes that are different. Unless these attitudes are addressed directly, they will create tension and unhappiness.

The solution is to discuss thoroughly the problem without resorting to name-calling or disrespectful language. And then come to a negotiated settlement. In this case, it might mean that you tell Barrie directly that he needs to be more aware of how his witty comments can hurt other people. And it may also mean not inviting Barrie to the party.

It might sound simplistic to insist that everyone is inevitably restricted by personal limitations. But, in fact, few of us ever consider how powerfully personal limitations affect us all. And we rarely acknowledge these limitations *before* we take an action or blast someone (or ourselves) with criticism, accusation, punishment or humiliation.

Wrapping It Up and Taking It Home

The sixty scenes in this book have emphasized several basic ideas that are fundamental to successful communication . . . and to success in life. Here's a brief review.

The overriding message in *Say This, Not That* is to practice thoughtfulness and strategic thinking. Thinking strategically doesn't come naturally to most of us. It requires attention—specifically, to your long-term best interests.

The goal of strategic thinking and speaking is to avoid provoking a Reactive Response in the listener or yourself, which in turn can set off escalating rounds of reaction.

Asking yourself *"What do I want to accomplish?"* before uttering any words to anyone is the broadest and most penetrating approach you can use when searching for the answer. *"How will my words influence my relationship with this person?"* is an equally helpful inquiry.

We've also covered the basic strategy of practicing *thoughtful silence*. This is not the same as "stonewalling"—withdrawing into a stony coldness or hostile muteness. Rather, thoughtful silence involves maintaining eye contact and a neutral facial expression *while thinking about the best way to respond.*

And we've reviewed the benefit of simply nodding your head, when appropriate, to show interest or saying, "Uh huh," while keeping a neutral expression. This invites the other person to continue speaking because it's obvious that you're paying attention. It's a highly effective strategy because you're not taking a risk by saying something inappropriate. Instead, you're giving yourself time to figure out where the discussion is going and deciding what you want to accomplish.

Saying the most effective words in the right moment is a skill that can be learned. And once you've successfully chosen effective words and watched other people respond positively a number of times, those successes will reinforce your resolve to master the same skill in a wider set of situations.

I recently watched an interview with the CEO of an international nonprofit, an Englishman known for his successful diplomacy in numerous stressful situations.

The interviewer asked him a tricky personal question: "How would you respond if your wife asked, 'Does this dress look good on me?'" Without pause, he replied, "I'd say, 'Darling, you look marvelous.'"

"But suppose the dress didn't look good. Would you lie to her?"

"I never forget my goal," the CEO replied. "With my wife, it's to please her." He smiled artfully. "Fortunately, beauty is in the eye of the beholder. I never forget that, either."

Now, there's someone who has deeply absorbed the skills of thinking and speaking strategically.

It's a skill—and an art—that's available to anyone who studies it.

I wish you success in your studies.

ALSO BY CARL ALASKO

"Carl Alasko uncovers the traps that kill relationships, and offers a wide range of examples and solutions to enhance our connections with one another."

—JUDY TATELBAUM, L.C.S.W.,
author of *The Courage to Grieve* and *You Don't Have to Suffer*

978-1-58542-666-9
$14.95

BEYOND BLAME

Eliminating the
**Most Toxic
Form of BS
from Your Life**

Carl Alasko, author of *Emotional Bullshit*

This inspiring book reveals why no one is to blame—but everyone's accountable. Alasko teaches us to recognize the destruction
that blame causes in our lives—oftentimes without our even being
aware—and to put an end to it once and for all.

978-1-58542-876-2

$15.95

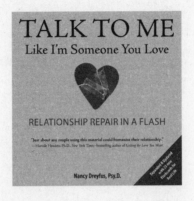

Expanded & Updated

"The most crucial relationship advice book since
Men Are from Mars."—ERIN MEANLEY, Glamour.com

978-0-399-16200-8

$17.95

If you enjoyed this book, visit

www.tarcherbooks.com

and sign up for Tarcher's e-newsletter to receive special offers, giveaway promotions, and information on hot upcoming releases.

TARCHER
PENGUIN

Great Lives Begin with Great Ideas

Connect with the Tarcher Community

. . .

Stay in touch with favorite authors!
Enter weekly contests!
Read exclusive excerpts!
Voice your opinions!

Follow us

 Tarcher Books

 @TarcherBooks

If you would like to place a bulk order
of this book, call 1-800-847-5515.